CliffsN

D0444125

The Catcher in the Rye

By Stanley P. Baldwin, M.A.

IN THIS BOOK

- Learn about the Life and Background of the Author
- Preview an Introduction to the Novel
- Explore themes, character development, and recurring images in the Critical Commentaries
- Examine in-depth Character Analyses
- Acquire an understanding of the novel with Critical Essays
- Reinforce what you learn with CliffsNotes Review
- Find additional information to further your study in the CliffsNotes Resource Center and online at www.cliffsnotes.com

Wiley Publishing, Inc.

About the Author

Stanley P. Baldwin received his M.A. in English from the University of Kentucky. He is a writer and teacher living in Nebraska.

Publisher's Acknowledgments

Editorial

Project Editor: Elizabeth Netedu Kuball
Acquisitions Editor: Gregory W. Tubach
Editorial Administrator: Michelle Hacker
Glossary Editors: The editors and staff of Webster's New World Dictionaries

Composition

Indexer: York Production Services, Inc.
Proofreader: York Production Services, Inc.
Wiley Indianapolis Composition Services

CliffsNotes™ *The Catcher in the Rye*

Published by:
Wiley Publishing, Inc.
111 River Street
Hoboken, N.J., 07030
www.wiley.com

Copyright © 2000 Wiley Publishing, Inc., Hoboken, N.J.
ISBN: 978-0-7645-8591-3
Printed in the United States of America
19 18 17 16 15 14 13 12
1O/RV/RQ/QS/IN
Published by Wiley Publishing, Inc., Hoboken, N.J.
Published simultaneously in Canada

Library of Congress Cataloging-in-Publication Data
Baldwin, Stanley P.
    CliffsNotes Salinger's The Catcher in the Rye / Stanley P. Baldwin
        p. cm.
    Includes index.
    ISBN 978-0-7645-8591-3 (alk. paper)
    1. Salinger, J.D. (Jerome David), 1919- Catcher in the Rye--Examinations--Study guides. 2. Caulfield, Holden (Fictitious character) 3. Runaway teenagers in literature. 4. Teenage boys in literature.   I. Title: The Catcher in the Rye. II Title.
PS3537.A426 C322 2000
813.54--dc21   00–039688
                                                                         CIP

For general information on our other products and services or to obtain technical support, please contact our Customer Care Department within the U.S. at 800-762-2974, outside the U.S. at 317-572-3993, or fax 317-572-4002.

Wiley also publishes its books in a variety of electronic formats. Some content that appears in print may not be available in electronic books.

Table of Contents

Life and Background of the Author 1
  Personal Background 2
  Career Highlights 3

Introduction to the Novel 7
  Historical Setting 8
  The Novel's Reception and Reputation 12
  A Brief Synopsis 14
  List of Characters 16
  Character Map 19

Critical Commentaries 21
  Chapter 1 22
    Summary 22
    Commentary 22
    Glossary 24
  Chapter 2 25
    Summary 25
    Commentary 25
    Glossary 26
  Chapter 3 28
    Summary 28
    Commentary 28
    Glossary 30
  Chapter 4 31
    Summary 31
    Commentary 31
    Glossary 32
  Chapter 5 33
    Summary 33
    Commentary 33
    Glossary 34
  Chapters 6 and 7 35
    Summary 35
    Commentary 35
    Glossary 36
  Chapters 8 and 9 37
    Summary 37
    Commentary 37
    Glossary 39

Chapter 10 41
 Summary 41
 Commentary 41
 Glossary 42
Chapter 11 43
 Summary 43
 Commentary 43
 Glossary 44
Chapter 12 45
 Summary 45
 Commentary 45
 Glossary 46
Chapter 13 47
 Summary 47
 Commentary 47
 Glossary 48
Chapter 14 49
 Summary 49
 Commentary 49
 Glossary 50
Chapter 15 51
 Summary 51
 Commentary 51
 Glossary 52
Chapter 16 53
 Summary 53
 Commentary 53
 Glossary 55
Chapter 17 56
 Summary 56
 Commentary 56
 Glossary 58
Chapters 18 and 19 59
 Summary 59
 Commentary 59
 Glossary 60
Chapter 20 61
 Summary 61
 Commentary 61
 Glossary 62

Chapter 21 63
   Summary 63
   Commentary 63
   Glossary 64
Chapter 22 65
   Summary 65
   Commentary 65
   Glossary 67
Chapter 23 68
   Summary 68
   Commentary 68
   Glossary 69
Chapter 24 70
   Summary 70
   Commentary 70
   Glossary 72
Chapters 25 and 26 73
   Summary 73
   Commentary 73
   Glossary 75

Character Analyses **77**
   Holden 78
   Phoebe 80
   Allie 81
   D.B. 82
   Mr. Antolini 83

Critical Essays **85**
   The Major Themes of *The Catcher in the Rye* .86
   Major Symbols of *The Catcher in the Rye* 89
   The Coming-of-Age Genre 91

CliffsNotes Review **93**

CliffsNotes Resource Center **96**

Index **99**

How to Use This Book

This CliffsNotes study guide on Salinger's *The Catcher in the Rye* supplements the original literary work, giving you background information about the author, an introduction to the work, a graphical character map, critical commentaries, expanded glossaries, and a comprehensive index, all for you to use as an educational tool that will allow you to better understand *The Catcher in the Rye*. This study guide was written with the assumption that you have read *The Catcher in the Rye*. Reading a literary work doesn't mean that you immediately grasp the major themes and devices used by the author; this study guide will help supplement your reading to be sure you get all you can from Salinger's *The Catcher in the Rye*. CliffsNotes Review tests your comprehension of the original text and reinforces learning with questions and answers, practice projects, and more. For further information on Jerome David (J.D.) Salinger and *The Catcher in the Rye*, check out the CliffsNotes Resource Center.

CliffsNotes provides the following icons to highlight essential elements of particular interest:

Reveals the underlying themes in the work.

Helps you to more easily relate to or discover the depth of a character.

Uncovers elements such as setting, atmosphere, mystery, passion, violence, irony, symbolism, tragedy, foreshadowing, and satire.

Enables you to appreciate the nuances of words and phrases.

Don't Miss Our Web Site

Discover classic literature as well as modern-day treasures by visiting the Cliffs Notes Web site at www.cliffsnotes.com. You can obtain a quick download of a CliffsNotes title, purchase a title in print form, browse our catalog, or view online samples.

You'll also find interactive tools that are fun and informative, links to interesting Web sites, tips, articles, and additional resources to help you, not only for literature, but for test prep, finance, careers, computers, and Internet too. See you at www.cliffsnotes.com!

LIFE AND BACKGROUND OF THE AUTHOR

The following abbreviated biography of J.D. Salinger is provided so that you might become more familiar with his life and the historical times that possibly influenced his writing. Read this Life and Background of the Author section and recall it when reading Salinger's *The Catcher in the Rye*, thinking of any thematic relationship between Salinger's work and his life.

Personal Background 2

Career Highlights 3

Personal Background

Jerome David (J.D.) Salinger, whose nickname as a child was "Sonny," was born on New Year's Day 1919, in New York, New York, the second and last child of Sol and Marie (Miriam) Jillich Salinger. He had a sister, Doris, eight years older. Salinger's father, a successful importer of meats and cheeses, was Jewish, his mother Scotch-Irish. Like most of Salinger's central characters, the family lived in the relative comfort of the upper-middle class.

Education

Young Salinger's early ambition was in dramatics; he was voted "most popular actor" at Camp Wigwam in Harrison, Maine, in the summer of 1930. An average student in public school on the Upper West Side in Manhattan, he was reported to be a quiet, polite, somewhat solitary child. His parents enrolled him in McBurney School in Manhattan in 1932, but he did not adjust well to the private school and struggled with grades. Concerned about their son's academic performance, his parents sent him to Valley Forge Military Academy in Pennsylvania when he was 15 years old. There, he was active in drama and singing clubs. He sometimes wrote fiction by flashlight under his blankets at night and contributed to the school's literary magazine. As editor of the academy's yearbook, *Crossed Sabres*, he published a poem in it that became the lyrics to the school's anthem. He graduated from Valley Forge Military Academy in June of 1936.

Salinger's collegiate experience was brief but significant. He attended New York University following prep school but withdrew to try performing as an entertainer on a Caribbean cruise ship. His father tried, in vain, to interest Salinger in the import business during a trip to Europe in 1937. Returning to school at Ursinus College in Collegetown, Pennsylvania, in 1938, Salinger wrote a column of humor, satire, and film reviews, called "Skipped Diploma," for the college newspaper.

At the age of 20, in 1939, Salinger enrolled in a short-story writing course at Columbia University taught by Whit Burnett, a writer and important editor; Salinger sold his first story to Burnett's *Story* magazine for twenty-five dollars the next year. Salinger published a grateful tribute to Burnett in *Fiction Writers' Hand-book* in 1975.

Early Work

Despite receiving a number of rejection slips, Salinger continued to write and submit stories. He sold his first Holden Caulfield story (eventually revised and titled "Slight Rebellion Off Madison") to the prestigious *New Yorker* magazine in 1941, but it was not published until 1946.

During the war, Salinger served as an enlisted man, reaching the rank of sergeant, and continued writing. He received counterintelligence training and landed on Utah Beach, Normandy, on D-day (June 6, 1944). Sergeant Salinger participated in five campaigns in Europe, witnessing some of the heaviest fighting in the war. He carried a portable typewriter in his jeep, serving his apprenticeship through commercially successful (if mostly forgettable) stories published in popular magazines such as *Cosmopolitan, Saturday Evening Post,* and *Esquire.* "I'm Crazy," appearing in *Collier's* magazine in 1945, included material later used in *The Catcher in the Rye.* But for the most part, Salinger tried to dissuade any republishing of these works. As he said in a rare interview with the *New York Times* in 1974, he preferred that such inferior efforts "die a perfectly natural death." A two-volume pirated edition of uncollected pieces did appear in 1974 despite the best efforts of Salinger and his attorney.

In 1946, a ninety-page novella (a short novel) about Holden Caulfield was nearly published, but Salinger withdrew from the agreement. Another five years passed before he introduced the classic in novel form.

In September of 1945, while still in Europe immediately following the war, Salinger apparently married a French professional, perhaps a physician, named Sylvia (whose maiden name is unknown). A divorce was granted in 1947. He married Claire Douglas on February 17, 1955. The couple had a daughter, Margaret Ann, and a son, Matthew, but divorced in 1967.

Career Highlights

Salinger published seven stories in the *New Yorker* between 1946 and 1951, developing a *first rejection rights* association (meaning the magazine had the first chance at publishing, or rejecting, his work) with the premiere magazine for serious writers. In 1948, "A Perfect Day for Bananafish" introduced Seymour Glass, perhaps the core character of the Glass stories and a figure whom some consider to be nearly as important as Holden in Salinger's work. Esteemed Salinger critic Warren French considers the story to be one of the more significant in American fiction since World War II.

The Success of *The Catcher in the Rye*

After a gestation period of ten years, *The Catcher in the Rye* was published on July 16, 1951, changing American fiction and J.D. Salinger's life. As French points out, Salinger was "unprepared for the kind of cult success" brought by the novel. The author progressively became one of the most famous of literary recluses, moving to Cornish, New Hampshire, in 1953 and rarely granting interviews or making public appearances. He found fame abhorrent and literary criticism distasteful.

When Ian Hamilton attempted an unauthorized biography of J.D. Salinger in the 1980s, Salinger successfully protested the use of letters that he had written to friends and editors between 1939 and 1961. He claimed infringement of copyright and invasion of privacy even though the letters had been donated to libraries and were available for study. A Federal Appeals Court denied use of even short quotations or paraphrases from the letters. Salinger was granted legal injunctions against publication of Hamilton's book; these were upheld when the United States Supreme Court refused to review the verdicts of two lower federal courts that held in favor of Salinger. The decision was considered extraordinary. According to David Margolic, legal affairs writer for the *New York Times*, this was "the first time in American memory that a book had been enjoined prior to publication, and it sent shock waves throughout the academic and publishing communities" (November 1, 1987).

Short Stories

For a time, Salinger continued to publish. His short story "Franny" appeared in the January 29, 1955, issue of the *New Yorker*. Franny is the youngest of the Glass daughters. She is confused by her desire for a spiritual relationship and her physical, sexual involvement with a crude boyfriend. The May 4, 1957, *New Yorker* carried a companion piece, "Zooey," in which Franny's older brother guides her while discovering his own spiritual awareness. "Raise High the Roof Beam, Carpenters" (1955) is Buddy Glass's recollection of Seymour's scheduled wedding and the reactions of the guests when the groom failed to attend. "Seymour: An Introduction" (1959) offers Buddy's attempt to explain Seymour to the general reader.

"Hapworth 16, 1924" (in the *New Yorker* on June 19, 1965) was Salinger's last publication for many years. In early 1997, however, Salinger's representatives announced that Orchises Press in Alexandria, Virginia, would publish this novella in book form. The story consists of a long letter from Seymour Glass to his family, concerning his experiences at summer camp at the age of seven.

In 1998, Joyce Maynard published a memoir (*At Home in the World*) recalling her 1972 affair, at the age of 18, with J.D. Salinger. Along with numerous bizarre details, she reports that the author had two completed, unpublished novels kept in a vault.

Published Works

In addition to *The Catcher in the Rye* (1951), Salinger has published, in book form, a well-received collection, *Nine Stories* (1953); *Franny and Zooey* (1961) as companion pieces; and two related Glass stories, *Raise High the Roof Beam, Carpenters*, and *Seymour: An Introduction* (1963). An unauthorized edition, *The Complete Uncollected Short Stories of J.D. Salinger*, appeared in two volumes between 1967 and 1974.

In 1950, Samuel Goldwyn Studio released a motion picture, *My Foolish Heart*, based on "Uncle Wiggily in Connecticut" (published in the *New Yorker* in 1948). Although the film received generally favorable reviews, Salinger reportedly was so upset by the distortion of his theme that he vowed never to allow Hollywood to get hold of another piece of his work.

INTRODUCTION TO THE NOVEL

The following Introduction section is provided solely as an educational tool and is not meant to replace the experience of your reading the work. Read the Introduction and A Brief Synopsis to enhance your understanding of the work and to prepare yourself for the critical thinking that should take place whenever you read any work of fiction or nonfiction. Keep the List of Characters and Character Map at hand so that as you read the original literary work, if you encounter a character about whom you're uncertain, you can refer to the List of Characters and Character Map to refresh your memory.

Historical Setting .8

The Novel's Reception and Reputation .12

A Brief Synopsis .14

List of Characters 16

Character Map .19

Historical Setting

Holden Caulfield's America was a nation of contrasts. World War II was over, and the boys had come home, but to what? Financially, life had improved significantly for the average worker since the Great Depression of the 1930s, but inflation presented new problems. The political scene generally moved toward conservatism near the end of the 1940s and into the 1950s (the time period of the novel), but there were noteworthy exceptions. The atomic bomb, which many had considered a blessing when it quickly ended the war with Japan, was increasingly seen as a curse. Culturally, the United States was both conservative and liberal but leaning increasingly to the right.

Economy

The economy had certainly improved since the 1930s. The New Deal programs of President Franklin D. Roosevelt (thirty-second President of the United States, serving from 1933–1945) combined with the enormous financial boost of World War II to pull the United States out of the nightmare of the Great Depression. Between 1941 and 1945, the years of America's involvement in the war, average individual weekly earnings had increased from $24.20 to $44.39. Workers faced a full-time workweek of forty-eight hours, but that would soon be reduced to a forty-hour week, often with no loss of pay, following an example set by the federal government.

Women had contributed significantly to the war effort by filling jobs in industry as well as serving in the armed forces. Some chose to continue with professional careers, an important step in the emancipation of women in the twentieth century. Others chose to return to traditional roles as housewives, opening more jobs for the returning men. This process took time, and the wait was difficult for many individuals. The strain was buffered by the GI Bill but exacerbated by inflation.

The GI Bill of Rights provided educational and other financial opportunities for returning members of the armed forces. Literally tens of thousands of service personnel, who otherwise would not have been able to afford it, attended college. A serious problem, however, was inflation. During the war, the emergency Office of Price Administration had kept costs in check. After its elimination, inflation ran rampant. In some areas, food prices doubled within a month. The cost of living rose by a third. Those on a fixed income, including many attending schools on the GI Bill, were especially strained.

In *The Catcher in the Rye*, Holden's family, and the families of the boys with whom Holden attends school, appear to have no financial concerns. Holden's family lives in an expensive apartment in an affluent section of New York City. Holden's father is a corporate attorney. Holden assures us that all a lawyer does is "make a lot of dough and play golf and play bridge and buy cars and drink Martinis and look like a hot-shot." (Chapter 22) Although his profession is probably more difficult than what his son makes it out to be, Mr. Caulfield is doing very well financially. He can afford a live-in maid, Charlene, and his son seems to go from one private school to another with little concern for cost. Holden's perspective is that of the upper-middle class. In the first chapter of the novel, he notices that the Spencers, whom he is visiting, can't afford a maid and have to answer their door themselves—"They didn't have too much dough"—indicating Holden's socioeconomic background.

Politics

Politically, the United States was becoming increasingly conservative. In 1948, Harry S Truman, a Roosevelt liberal from Missouri, who never attended college and had gone through bankruptcy, defeated conservative Thomas Edmund Dewey, an attorney with degrees from the University of Michigan and Columbia University, for the office of President of the United States. Although Truman had been Roosevelt's vice president and held the office since FDR's death in 1945, his victory shocked the experts. Four years later, Republican conservative General Dwight Eisenhower won easily, as he would again in 1956. Other factors affected these elections, but the shift toward conservatism was paramount.

In February of 1950, a first-term U.S. Senator from Wisconsin named Joseph McCarthy accused the Department of State of employing 205 known Communists. He later reduced the number to 57. Although the accusations were never proven, McCarthy had become a national figure and the most infamous leader of a witch-hunt that rivaled that of Salem in 1692.

In the early 1950s, as head of the Senate subcommittee on investigations, McCarthy expanded his search for Communist influence, which contributed to what historian William Manchester (author of *The Glory and the Dream: A Narrative History of American, 1932–1972*, published by Bantam Books) titled "the age of suspicion." Blacklists, banning the accused from employment, appeared across the country. State legislatures demanded that college professors, a typically liberal group, for example, sign loyalty oaths pledging their allegiance to the United States and disavowing any association with Communism. The University of California at Los Angeles (UCLA) fired 157 professors who protested that such an oath was unconstitutional. In the entertainment industry, another predominantly liberal group, some writers, directors, and actors were blacklisted for years, their careers ruined. Good reasons to be concerned about spies did exist in this time period, but too often the wrong people were accused.

This spirit of repression is the context in which *The Catcher in the Rye* appeared. When the novel has been banned from classrooms, it has been because school boards and administrators have objected to the language as well as the general atmosphere of subversion in the book. Officials at a high school in Nebraska (one example of many) feared that the old Pencey alum, who wants to see if his initials are still carved in a dormitory bathroom door (in Chapter 22), might encourage vandalism. *The Christian Science Monitor* (July 19, 1951) concluded that the novel was "not fit for children to read" and that Holden Caulfield was "preposterous, profane, and pathetic beyond belief." Ironically, Holden himself is opposed to the strongest obscenity in the novel and the vandalism that produces it. As C.V. Xiong pointed out in a lecture at Creighton University (spring 1999), the novel remains near the top of the list of banned books in public libraries in America, especially in rural areas. Reasons cited continue to be language, subversive concepts, and parental disapproval.

Nuclear Threat

When the Soviet Union set off its first nuclear explosion in 1949, it was clear that the cold war could turn hot and destroy civilization. A real fear permeated American culture. Even in remote areas, ordinary people built bomb shelters in their backyards. Schools took time to instruct students on the best way to react during a nuclear attack. Although the intent was benevolent, the most likely result was fear and confusion on the part of impressionable young minds. This increased gap between adult values and childhood innocence may have affected Salinger and certainly affected his audience. Whatever Holden's politics might have been, many readers related to his resentment of the insensitive, cruel, and phony elements of life.

Milieu

Culturally, society was moving toward conservatism but with important pockets of resistance. In 1949, the first nationally recognized, uniform suburban communities appeared, called *Levittowns*, after designer William J. Levitt. We can guess what Holden would say about them. Flying saucers were first reported that year (Holden may have found these more interesting). China became Red China in 1949. Closer to home, Billy Graham, an American evangelist, began his first large-scale Christian crusade. Veterans of World War II had mixed feelings of disillusionment and hope, echoed by Salinger and embodied, however subconsciously, in Holden.

In contrast to the affluence and conformity of the time were the "beats." First noticed in the coffeehouses of Los Angeles, New York, and San Francisco in the early 1950s and soon centered in poet and co-owner Lawrence Ferlinghetti's City Lights Bookshop in San Francisco, the beats were the flip side of suburbia. They advocated individuality, poetry, jazz music, Zen Buddhism, and such controversial lifestyle choices as free love and smoking pot. Some of the best known were Jack Kerouac, a merchant seaman during the war and author of the beat classic *On the Road* (1957); Allen Ginsberg, a former market research consultant and author of *Howl* (1956); former popcorn salesman turned poet, Kenneth Rexroth; and William S. Burroughs, outspoken drug addict and author of *The Naked Lunch* (published in Paris in 1959 and in the U. S. as *Naked Lunch* in 1962). The term *beat* implies weary, defeated, and hip to the rhythms of poetry and jazz. Like Holden Caulfield, the narrator of *The Catcher in the Rye*, the beats probably would prefer something other than Radio City Music Hall or Ernie's Nightclub. Several of the beats had been through psychotherapy, and Ginsberg famously wrote that he had seen the "best minds of [his] generation" destroyed by madness. It could be argued that, after his release from the mental hospital, Holden might be just about ready to join this important movement.

Polio

During this same period, in 1949, scientists, led by a bacteriologist named John Franklin Enders, developed a method of growing poliomyelitis viruses in a laboratory, leading to Jonas Salk's successful polio vaccine five years later. That was followed by Albert Sabin's oral vaccine. Sometimes called "infantile paralysis," the disabling, often paralyzing disease hit children hardest. In 1952, there were 57,879 new cases of polio reported in the United States. With routine immunization, there would be only a few cases ten years later. In Chapter 24 of *The Catcher in the Rye*, Holden recalls a speech student at Pencey Prep, a boy named Richard Kinsella, whose consideration of his polio-infected uncle was interesting to Holden but condemned as a "digression" by fellow students and the instructor. Readers in the early 1950s would understand the terror and destruction that polio produced.

Manhattan

New York City itself was a lighter, safer, less hostile place for Holden than it has been for some subsequent generations. Central Park was a gathering place for families. However, there *is* an undercurrent of fear, danger, and decadence, centered in New York City, that Holden seems both repelled by and attracted to. *The Catcher in the Rye* appeals to us because of its universality, but it is important that it takes place mostly in Manhattan at the crossroads of the 1940s and 1950s. As Sanford Pinsker points out in *The Catcher in the Rye: Innocence Under Pressure* (published by Simon & Schuster), the novel is a "mixture of bright talk and brittle manners, religious quest and nervous breakdown, [which] captured not only the perennial confusions of adolescence, but also the spiritual discomforts of an entire age."

The Novel's Reception and Reputation

In retrospect, it might be easy to assume that *The Catcher in the Rye* was an immediate smash hit, critically and commercially, when it was published by Little, Brown and Company on July 16, 1951. In fact, the reviews were mixed. Although the book sold well, it was not an overwhelming sensation and never reached number one on the best-seller lists. The unusual thing about Salinger's first novel is its staying power.

Many of the novel's early reviews were favorable. On July 14, 1951, the *Saturday Review* praised the work as "remarkable" and "absorbing." Given Salinger's affiliation with the *New Yorker* magazine, we might expect extensive attention from that publication, and such was the case; S. N. Behrman wrote an unusually long and strong review (August 11, 1951), stressing the personal attraction of Phoebe and Holden as characters. The Book-of-the-Month Club selected the novel as a summer alternate, assuring significant sales and widespread attention. In the

Book-of-the-Month Club News (July 1951), its large membership received a very positive review by the respected literary critic Clifton Fadiman, including one of the most widely quoted early comments on Holden Caulfield: "[T]hat rare miracle of fiction has again come to pass: a human being has been created out of ink, paper, and the imagination."

Other critics hedged their bets. An unsigned review in the July 15, 1951, *Booklist* found the work "imaginative" but warned of "coarse language." Writing for the *Library Journal* (July 1951), Harold L. Roth "highly recommended" the novel but warned that it "may be a shock to many parents" and should be thought of as strictly *adult* reading. The reviewer for the *Nation* (September 1, 1951) liked parts of the story but generally thought it was "predictable and boring." Anne L. Goodman of the *New Republic* (July 16, 1951) rated the final (carrousel) scene "as good as anything that Salinger has written" but concluded that "the book as a whole is disappointing"; there was just too much of Holden in the book for her. In the August 1951 *Atlantic Monthly*, Harvey Breit considered the work as a "summer novel" and found it to be a "near miss" in effectiveness. He was, however, one of the first to compare *The Catcher in the Rye* to Mark Twain's *The Adventures of Huckleberry Finn*, an insight whose value has held up over time. In the July 15, 1951, *New York Times*, James Stern chose an approach that, unfortunately, was popular nationwide. Attempting to review the novel in the voice of its narrator, he offered such strained turns as, "This Salinger, he's a short-story guy. And he knows how to write about kids. This book though, it's too long. Gets kind of monotonous."

Still others condemned the novel. *The Christian Science Monitor* (July 19, 1951) complained of the "wholly repellent" vulgarity and "sly perversion" of the piece, concluding that no one who truly loved children could have written such a work. In another widely quoted assessment, *Catholic World* (November 1951) complained about the "excessive use of amateur swearing and coarse language" and suggested that "some of the events stretch probability," calling Holden "monotonous and phony."

British reviewers were generally unimpressed. *The Spectator* (August 17, 1951) considered it to be "inconclusive" in theme and a bit too "showy." *Times Literary Supplement* (September 7, 1951) complains that the "endless stream of blasphemy and obscenity" gets boring after the first chapter.

The novel did well commercially but was not the most popular work of fiction in 1951. It was on the *New York Times* best-seller list for thirty weeks in all but never climbed higher than fourth. Herman Wouk's *The*

Caine Mutiny and James Jones' *From Here to Eternity*, for example, sold more copies initially.

As time passed, however, Salinger's work continued to sell and to attract critical interest. Jack Salzman (in *New Essays on The Catcher in the Rye*, published by Cambridge University Press) points out that, by 1954, *Catcher* could be purchased in translation in Denmark, Germany, France, Israel, Italy, Japan, Sweden, Switzerland, and the Netherlands. That international popularity is especially interesting considering the novel's dependence on the vernacular. The American version sold 1.5 million copies, mostly in paperback, within its first ten years. Eudora Welty (*New York Times*, April 5, 1953) gave Salinger a critical boost in a very favorable review of his collection, *Nine Stories*. James E. Miller (*J.D. Salinger*, 1965) was an important, relatively early supporter. Literally scores of critical works have praised, scrutinized, and dissected the novel.

There have been, of course, those with reservations. In 1959, Norman Mailer (*Advertisements for Myself*, published by Harvard University Press) called Salinger "the greatest mind to ever stay in prep school." In the August 1961 *Atlantic Monthly*, Alfred Kazin sardonically referred to the author as "everybody's favorite" and disparagingly classified Holden as *cute*: "cute in his little-boy suffering for his dead brother, Allie, and cute in his tenderness for his sister, 'Old Phoebe.'" Writing for the *Saturday Review* (October 1, 1960), Harvey Swados commented on Salinger's obsession with privacy by dubbing him the "Greta Garbo of American letters"; he found the author talented but boring. Swados and others seem to resent Salinger's popularity, which they attribute to a "cult of personality."

The continuing appeal of *The Catcher in the Rye* can be traced to two factors. First, it is superbly written. Even Salinger's critics usually admit that he captures the vernacular of the prep school adolescent of the time. Second, the novel's insight appeals to the young, the young at heart, the dreamers of succeeding generations and various cultures. On that rest its universality and its staying power.

A Brief Synopsis

Holden Caulfield, the seventeen-year-old narrator and protagonist of the novel, addresses the reader directly from a mental hospital or sanitarium in southern California. He wants to tell us about events that took place over a two-day period the previous December. Typically, he first digresses to mention his older brother, D.B., who was once a "terrific" short-story writer but now has sold out and writes scripts in nearby Hollywood. The body of the novel follows. It is a *frame story*, or long flashback, constructed through Holden's memory.

Holden begins at Pencey Prep, an exclusive private school in Pennsylvania, on the Saturday afternoon of the traditional football game with school rival, Saxon Hall. Holden misses the game. Manager of the fencing team, he managed to lose the team's equipment on the subway that morning, resulting in the cancellation of a match in New York. He is on his way to the home of his history teacher, Mr. Spencer, to say goodbye. Holden has been expelled and is not to return after Christmas break, which begins Wednesday.

Spencer is a well-meaning but long-winded old man, and Holden gladly escapes to the quiet of an almost deserted dorm. Wearing his new red hunting cap, he begins to read. His reverie is temporary. First, a dorm neighbor named Ackley disturbs him. Later, Holden argues with his roommate, Stradlater, who fails to appreciate a theme that Holden has written for him about Holden's deceased brother Allie's baseball glove. A womanizer, Stradlater has just returned from a date with Holden's old friend Jane Gallagher. The two roommates fight, Stradlater winning easily. Holden has had enough of Pencey Prep and catches a train to New York City where he plans to stay in a hotel until Wednesday, when his parents expect him to return home for Christmas vacation.

En route to New York, Holden meets the mother of a Pencey classmate and severely distorts the truth by telling her what a popular boy her "rat" son is. Holden's Manhattan hotel room faces windows of another wing of the hotel, and he observes assorted behavior by "perverts." Holden struggles with his own sexuality. He meets three women in their thirties, tourists from Seattle, in the hotel lounge and enjoys dancing with one but ends up with only the check. Following a disappointing visit to Ernie's Nightclub in Greenwich Village, Holden agrees to have a prostitute, Sunny, visit his room. Holden has second thoughts, makes up an excuse, and pays the girl to leave. To his surprise, Maurice, her pimp, soon returns with her and beats up Holden for more money. He has lost two fights in one night. It is near dawn Sunday morning.

After a short sleep, Holden telephones Sally Hayes, a familiar date, and agrees to meet her that afternoon to go to a play. Meanwhile, Holden leaves the hotel, checks his luggage at Grand Central Station, and has a late breakfast. He meets two nuns, one an English teacher, with whom he discusses *Romeo and Juliet*. Holden looks for a special record for his 10-year-old sister, Phoebe, called "Little Shirley Beans." He spots a small boy singing "If a body catch a body coming through the rye," which somehow makes Holden feel less depressed.

Sally is snobbish and "phony," but the two watch a play featuring married Broadway stars Alfred Lunt and Lynn Fontanne. Sally and Holden skate at Radio City but fight when Holden tries to discuss things that really matter to him and suddenly suggests that they run off together. Holden leaves, sees the Christmas show at Radio City Music Hall, endures a movie, and gets very drunk. Throughout the novel, Holden has been worried about the ducks in the lagoon at Central Park. He tries to find them but only manages to break Phoebe's recording in the process. Exhausted physically and mentally, he heads home to see his sister.

Holden and Phoebe are close friends as well as siblings. He tells her that the one thing he'd like to be is "the catcher in the rye." He would stand near the edge of a cliff, by a field of rye, and catch any of the playing children who, in their abandon, come close to falling off. When his parents return from a late night out, Holden, undetected, leaves the apartment and visits the home of Mr. Antolini, a favorite teacher, where he hopes to stay a few days. Startled, Holden awakes in the predawn hours to find Antolini patting Holden's head. He quickly leaves.

Monday morning, Holden arranges to meet Phoebe for lunch. He plans to say good-bye and head west where he hopes to live as a deaf-mute. She insists on leaving with him, and he finally agrees to stay. Holden's story ends with Phoebe riding a carrousel in the rain as Holden watches.

In the final chapter, Holden is at the sanitarium in California. He doesn't want to tell us any more. In fact, the whole story has only made him miss people, even the jerks.

List of Characters

Holden The protagonist and narrator of the novel, he tells his story from a sanitarium in California.

Phoebe Holden's 10-year-old sister is his most trusted link to family.

Allie Holden's younger brother died on July 18, 1946, when he was 11 and Holden was 13. When he needs help, Holden sometimes speaks to Allie.

D.B. Holden feels that his older brother, once a terrific short-story writer, has now sold out to Hollywood by writing screenplays.

Mother Holden's mother appears briefly in Chapter 23 to check on Phoebe during Holden's secret visit.

Charlene The Caufield's maid.

Mr. Antolini Holden's favorite teacher while at Elkton Hills, he is now an English instructor at New York University. His behavior at the Antolinis' apartment disturbs Holden.

Lillian Antolini Serious, older, asthmatic, intellectual, and wealthy, Antolini's wife is a somewhat enigmatic partner for the popular young instructor.

Mr. Spencer An elderly history teacher at Pencey Prep, he may mean well but has a tendency toward pontificating.

Mrs. Spencer The history professor's wife is known for her forbearance, kindness, and hot chocolate.

Mr. Vinson Holden's speech teacher at Pencey wants his students to unify and simplify their speeches but never digress.

Sally Hayes Holden's date to a matinee on Sunday is attractive but shallow and artificial.

Jane Gallagher Holden likes to remember Jane as a sensitive, innocent girl with a unique approach to checkers. She is Stradlater's date Saturday evening, which bothers Holden.

Ward Stradlater Holden's roommate at Pencey is handsome but vain and a boorish womanizer.

Robert Ackley Holden's dorm neighbor at Pencey is a regular annoyance.

Ossenburger A wealthy alum, his hackneyed speech to the Pencey students at chapel is interrupted in a creative way by Edgar Marsalla. Holden's dorm wing is named after the mortician magnate.

James Castle A student at Elkton Hills, he jumped to his death rather than recant a statement about an arrogant bully.

Mrs. Morrow The mother of Holden's contemptible classmate, Ernest, she shares a train ride and creative conversation with "Rudolf Schmidt," the alias used by Holden.

Sunny A teenage prostitute at the Edmont Hotel, she is frightening despite her "little bitty voice."

Maurice To collect an extra five bucks, Sunny's pimp roughs up Holden, who is calling himself "Jim Steele" for the hooker.

Bernice, Marty, and Laverne Three thirtyish tourists from Seattle, they leave Holden with the tab at the Lavender Room. Bernice is a very good dancer.

Ernie A talented pianist at his own club in Greenwich Village, he exemplifies Holden's concept of an artist who has sold out.

Lillian Simmons All bust and no brains, she and her date ask Holden to sit with them at Ernie's. She used to date D.B. and oozes her fake charm in hopes of making a good impression.

Horwitz The most interesting of the cab drivers in the novel, he takes Holden to Ernie's Nightclub and offers unusual zoological insight regarding those ducks and the fish at the lagoon.

Faith Cavendish As one example of Holden's struggles with sexuality, she turns down his awkward and untimely request for a date.

Character Map

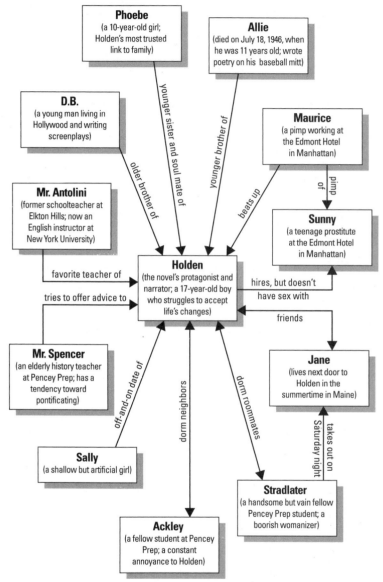

Phoebe (a 10-year-old girl; Holden's most trusted link to family)

Allie (died on July 18, 1946, when he was 11 years old; wrote poetry on his baseball mitt)

D.B. (a young man living in Hollywood and writing screenplays)

Maurice (a pimp working at the Edmont Hotel in Manhattan)

Mr. Antolini (former schoolteacher at Elkton Hills; now an English instructor at New York University)

Sunny (a teenage prostitute at the Edmont Hotel in Manhattan)

Mr. Spencer (an elderly history teacher at Pencey Prep; has a tendency toward pontificating)

Holden (the novel's protagonist and narrator; a 17-year-old boy who struggles to accept life's changes)

Jane (lives next door to Holden in the summertime in Maine)

Sally (a shallow but artificial girl)

Stradlater (a handsome but vain fellow Pencey Prep student; a boorish womanizer)

Ackley (a fellow student at Pencey Prep; a constant annoyance to Holden)

younger sister and soul mate of

younger brother of

older brother of

beats up

pimp of

favorite teacher of

tries to offer advice to

hires, but doesn't have sex with

friends

off-and-on date of

dorm neighbors

dorm roommates

takes out on Saturday night

CRITICAL COMMENTARIES

The sections that follow provide great tools for
supplementing your reading of *The Catcher in the Rye*.
First, in order to enhance your understanding of and
enjoyment from reading, we provide quick summaries in
case you have difficulty when you read the original
literary work. Each summary is followed by commentary:
literary devices, character analyses, themes, and so on.
Keep in mind that the interpretations here are solely
those of the author of this study guide and are used to
jumpstart your thinking about the work. No single interpretation of a complex work like *The Catcher in the Rye* is
infallible or exhaustive, and you'll likely find that you
interpret portions of the work differently from the author
of this study guide. Read the original work and
determine your own interpretations, referring to these
Notes for supplemental meanings only.

Chapter 1 22
Chapter 2 25
Chapter 3 28
Chapter 4 31
Chapter 5 33
Chapters 6 and 7 35
Chapters 8 and 9 37
Chapter 10 41
Chapter 11 43
Chapter 12 45
Chapter 13 47
Chapter 14 49
Chapter 15 51
Chapter 16 53
Chapter 17 56
Chapters 18 and 19 59
Chapter 20 61
Chapter 21 63
Chapter 22 65
Chapter 23 68
Chapter 24 70
Chapters 25 and 26 73

Chapter 1

Summary

As the novel opens, the narrator, Holden Caulfield, speaks directly to the reader from a mental hospital or sanitarium in southern California. He says that he will tell us (the readers) of events occurring around Christmastime of the previous year. First, however, he mentions his older brother, D.B., a writer who now works in nearby Hollywood and visits Holden nearly every weekend.

Holden's story, in the form of a long flashback, begins around 3 p.m. on a Saturday in December, the day of the traditional season-ending football match between his old school, Pencey Prep (in Agerstown, Pennsylvania) and rival Saxon Hall. Holden, a junior at Pencey, can see the field from where he stands, high atop Thomsen Hill. He has been expelled and is on his way to say good-bye to Mr. Spencer, his history instructor. At the end of the chapter, Holden arrives at Mr. Spencer's house and is let in by his teacher's wife.

Commentary

In one of the best-known openings in American fiction, Salinger sets the tone for Holden's personality and narrative style. The first paragraph of the novel is often compared to the opening lines of Mark Twain's novel *The Adventures of Huckleberry Finn* (1884). From the beginning, we, the readers, realize that Holden is not a traditional narrator. He eschews details about his birth, his parents, and "all that David Copperfield kind of crap" (referring to Charles Dickens' novel by the same name). Holden speaks in the vernacular of a teenager of his day (the late 1940s). The literary point of view is first-person singular, unique to Holden but easily accessible to the rebels, romantics, innocents, and dreamers of any generation.

After stating that he will just tell us about the "madman stuff" that happened the previous December, Holden typically digresses to describe his brother, D.B., who was a "terrific" short story writer until he sold out and went to Hollywood. The theme of Holden's favorite

D.B. story, "The Secret Goldfish" (about a child who buys a goldfish and does not allow anyone to look at it, because he has paid for it with his own money) foreshadows Holden's consistent passion for the innocence and authenticity of childhood.

Literary
Device

The setting for the early chapters in the flashback is Pencey Prep, a "terrible" school whose atmosphere seems as cold as the December air on Thomsen Hill. Holden has no love for prep schools. Although he oddly respects the academic standards of Pencey, he sees it as phony, if not evil. Magazine ads for the school, featuring horsemanship, are misleading because, Holden claims, he has never seen a horse anywhere near Pencey. The school's motto, concerned with molding boys into "splendid" young men, is "for the birds," according to Holden. After all, one of the students has stolen his winter coat and fur-lined gloves.

Character
Insight

Holden is not attending the football game for two reasons, both of which reveal a good deal about his character. First, Holden is careless and sometimes irresponsible. As manager of the fencing team, he left the equipment on the subway en route to a meet that morning with McBurney School in New York City. The team has returned to the school much earlier than it had planned. Second, Holden is on his way to bid farewell to his history teacher, Mr. Spencer, indicating that he *does* care about people. Holden has been expelled for academic failure and is not to return after Christmas break, which begins the following Wednesday. Even though he failed history with an abysmal performance, Holden does not blame the instructor. He likes old Spencer. Perhaps readers appreciate Holden more because he is not a perfect "hero." Certainly we are attracted to him because he has a heart.

Salinger himself was once enrolled in McBurney School in Manhattan, the intended site of the novel's canceled fencing meet. In addition, scholars often compare Pencey Prep to Valley Forge Military Academy, which Salinger attended from the ages of 15 to 17. Although similarities to Salinger's life occasionally occur throughout *The Catcher in the Rye*, as readers we should be careful about biographical interpretations. Writers often use personal experience as background. Holden may be a part of Salinger, but the first-person narrator should not be confused with the author.

Holden has been expelled from Pencey Prep because he has flunked four subjects (passing only English), including Mr. Spencer's history class. On his way to Spencer's home to say good-bye, Holden feels terribly cold. There is no sun, and he feels as though he might disappear as he crosses Route 204 to go to Spencer's house. This is the first of several instances when Holden feels he is losing himself or falling into an abyss. He arrives at the Spencer home frozen and shaken.

Glossary

(Here and in the following sections, difficult words and phrases are explained.)

David Copperfield the first-person narrator of *The Personal History of David Copperfield* by Charles Dickens, published serially 1849-50 and in book form 1850.

hemorrhage the escape of large quantities of blood from a blood vessel; heavy bleeding.

prostitute to sell (oneself, one's artistic or moral integrity, etc.) for low or unworthy purposes; here, one who compromises principle for money.

faggy fatigued; wearied.

falsies devices, as pads or breast-shaped forms, worn inside a brassiere to make the breasts look fuller.

ostracized banished, barred, excluded, etc. by general consent, as from a group or from acceptance by society.

grippe influenza; the flu.

t.b. tuberculosis (an infectious disease characterized by the formation of abnormal hard swellings in tissues of the body, especially in the lungs).

Chapter 2

Summary

Spencer's farewell turns into a lecture on discipline, and Holden's mind drifts. He wonders about the ducks down at the lagoon near Central Park South in New York City. Where do they go when the lagoon freezes in the winter? Does someone take them to a zoo? Do they fly away? He reflects on Mr. Haas, the phony headmaster at Elkton Hills, one of Holden's previous schools. Haas was very charming to successful-looking parents, but if a boy's mother were fat or his father poorly dressed, the headmaster snubbed them cruelly.

Holden finally manages to escape from Mr. Spencer's lecture, claiming he needs to get to the gym to retrieve his equipment. He has second thoughts about leaving "old Spencer" but mainly wants out. Politely turning down a cup of Mrs. Spencer's renowned hot chocolate and promising to write, he gladly leaves.

Commentary

Kindly Mrs. Spencer is the one who invites Holden into the couple's modest home and directs him toward the ailing instructor's bedroom. Holden's background is sufficiently privileged that he mentions the absence of servants to open the doors to visitors. The Spencers are an elderly couple, although we need to be cautious about specifics because Holden tends to exaggerate. He mentions several "old guy" habits that Mr. Spencer indulges in and a few other human failings that annoy him. Worst is the reading aloud of Holden's final exam from Spencer's history class.

Character Insight

Holden reveals flaws in his own character as well as condemning them in the rest of the world. He is 17 as he narrates the story and was 16 when the events took place, but he admits to behaving like a 12-year-old at times. He finds this especially ironic because he is 6 feet 2½ inches tall, having grown 6½ inches the previous year. The right side of Holden's head is covered with gray hair, another irony. He knows he should act more mature; his personal habits are poor at times, he smokes too much, he's a terrible liar, and he has trouble caring about school.

Hoping, in vain, to head off a lecture, Holden readily admits to Mr. Spencer that he rarely studied for history class, only glancing through the book a couple of times over the course of the semester. He knows he deserved to fail, which makes Spencer's harangue especially annoying. Holden rightly feels that it is a "dirty trick" when Spencer reads his exam aloud. It isn't as if the exam answer is news to Holden. He knows that the essay on Egyptians is "crap." Initially friendly, Holden is beginning to hate the old man.

Spencer exhibits several characteristics of older men, and Holden wonders why the teacher even bothers to continue living. Spencer yells instead of talking. He wraps himself in a beat-up Navajo blanket that he loves. His ratty bathrobe exposes legs that are too white and hairless. Spencer's chest is bumpy, and he picks his nose. He consistently misses as he tries to toss objects onto the nearby bed. When Spencer goes into his nodding routine, Holden doesn't know if it's because the old man is wisely thinking or because he "doesn't know his ass from his elbow."

Beneath all of the aggravation and age stereotyping, however, Holden often reveals his compassion. He sincerely cares about the ducks in Central Park. He sympathizes with the parents at Elkton Hills who were not attractive or fashionable and were objects of Haas' disdain. Even as he is trying to escape form Spencer's lecture, Holden feels "sorry as hell" for the teacher. He realizes that the old man genuinely cares about him. Holden ultimately thinks of the bathrobe as "sad" rather than "ratty," and he understands that the quirks are beyond Spencer's control. But Holden can't take it any longer. He and Spencer are, according to Holden, on "opposite ends of the pole," and he has to leave. We might suspect, also, that Holden feels uncomfortable when he sees some truth in Spencer's statements.

Glossary

Navajo North American Indian people who live in Arizona, New Mexico, and Utah.

Yellowstone Park national park mostly in northwestern Wyoming, but including narrow strips of southern Montana and eastern Idaho; it contains geysers, boilings springs, etc.

ratty shabby or run-down.

Beowulf hero of the Old English folk epic of that name, an Anglian poem probably composed during the first half of the 8th century, A.D.

Lord Randal My Son refers to an anonymous medieval ballad of northern England or Scotland.

chiffonier a narrow, high bureau or chest of drawers, often with a mirror.

Central Park popular, expansive public park in Manhattan, New York City.

qualms sudden feelings of uneasiness or doubt; misgivings; twinges of conscience.

Chapter 3

Summary

Holden returns to Pencey where he lives in the Ossenburger Memorial Wing of the new dorms, reserved for juniors and seniors. Ossenburger is an alumnus who has made a fortune in the undertaking business. Pencey named a wing of the new dormitories after him in thanks for a large donation. Ossenburger attended the first home football game earlier in the fall and bored the students, especially Holden, with a long-winded, corny, cliché-filled oration at chapel the next morning. A flatulent student named Edgar Marsalla finally countered with his own loud breaking of wind, much to Holden's delight.

The dorm room is empty and cozy. Holden tries on a red hunting cap, with a long bill, which he bought for a dollar in New York that morning. He relaxes with a good book, Isak Denisen's *Out of Africa*, until he is interrupted by Robert Ackley who rooms next door and enters through a shower that the two rooms share. Ackley is a nuisance and ruins the mood.

Ward Stradlater, Holden's roommate, comes in from the football game and asks to borrow Holden's hound's-tooth jacket as he prepares to go out for the evening.

Commentary

Literary Device

Ossenburger's character introduces the theme of death in a comic vein. The mortician is just the sort of establishment "phony" that Holden loves to mock. He has a chain of funeral parlors, profiting from high volume at low rates and, Holden is certain, shabby service. Ossenburger's speech at chapel is filled with "corny jokes" and clichés. He says that he is never ashamed to get down on his knees and talk to his buddy, Jesus. This humors Holden, who imagines Ossenburger asking Jesus to "send him a few more stiffs." Marsalla's magnificent fart, which, Holden reports, nearly "blew the roof off" the chapel, is the perfect response.

Holden opens the chapter by telling us that he loves to lie. It is unlikely that he is lying about that. Because he is the narrator, the reader might take some caution in "believing" what Holden says; he exaggerates mercilessly: Ossenburger's speech lasts ten hours, he tells us, flavored with fifty corny jokes; his cheap funerals probably consist of shoving the deceased into sacks and dumping them in a river; Ackley, the obnoxious pest next door, barges in on Holden about eighty-five times a day; Holden asks him not to clip his nails onto the floor fifty times. The world is not big enough for Holden; he needs to blow it up a little.

However, Holden's hyperbole and wild imaginings usually are not malicious. When he assumes a false identity or claims he is headed for the opera as he actually goes to buy a magazine, he is playing. Life is a bit boring for Holden; he just needs to liven up the action.

The red hunting cap is a strong symbol of Holden's unconventional joy. This is not a baseball cap. The bill is overly long. It is painfully unstylish, but Holden loves it. Unknowingly anticipating a style that would be popular several decades later, he wears it backward. Those who follow baseball can't help noticing that this is how a *catcher* wears his cap (a connection to the novel's title).

Holden also dons his unconventional cap indoors. Among other things, it is a reading cap for Holden. Perhaps the critics who say that Holden wears it backward because he is hunting himself are correct. More likely, Holden just loves the cap and enjoys being different.

Ackley is an excellent example of Salinger's skill at characterization. Numerous specifics reveal Ackley's personality. He is antisocial and cold to the point that even his wife, if he ever marries, will call him by his last name. He never brushes his teeth; they look "mossy and awful." He is nasty and hates everyone. He constantly disturbs Holden's personal belongings and puts them back in the wrong place.

In a distinct way, Holden differs from his creator. Ironically, when he reads a terrific book, Holden thinks it would be great to telephone the author and get to know him. They could become pals and talk whenever Holden feels like it. But it is safe to assume that J.D. Salinger, as an author, would not welcome such an invasion of his own privacy.

Glossary

sadist one who gets pleasure from inflicting physical or psychological pain on another or others.

wooden press here, a frame that holds a wooden tennis racket to prevent warping.

falsetto an artificial way of speaking, in which the voice is placed in a register much higher than that of the natural voice.

prince a fine, generous, helpful fellow.

hound's-tooth jacket a jacket featuring a pattern of irregular broken checks.

Chapter 4

Summary

Although the dorms have showers separating rooms, the toilets and sinks are down the hall. Having nothing better to do, Holden accompanies his roommate, Stradlater, as he prepares for a Saturday night date. Holden is first shocked and then concerned when he learns that his roommate's date that night is Jane Gallagher, a friend of his from the summer before his sophomore year. Holden repeatedly says he should go downstairs to say hello to Jane, but he never does.

Stradlater talks Holden into writing an English theme paper for him. Holden returns to his room and is joined by Ackley, whose company Holden doesn't mind, because listening to Ackley distracts him from thinking about Jane.

Commentary

Character Insight

Stradlater is a "Year Book kind of handsome guy." He has superficial good looks and is extremely photogenic, but he is arrogant and vain. He is also a secret slob. Stradlater may be well groomed, because he is in love with himself, but he lives like a pig. His razor, for example, is rusty and full of hair. He never cleans anything. He is a user—of women and of friends.

Stradlater wants Holden to compose a descriptive English theme for him because he knows that Holden writes well. Too lazy and incompetent to be a decent writer himself, Stradlater aggravates Holden by pretending that the only reason he can't write is that he puts the commas in the wrong places.

Holden has good reason to be concerned for Jean Stradlater is an experienced womanizer, and the Jean that Holden knows is an innocent dreamer, the kind of girl who, when she plays checkers, leaves her kings lined up in the opponent's back row, where they were crowned, preferring aesthetic design to victory. Holden's one consolation is that he knows Jean has already irked Stradlater by signing out of her dorm only until 9:30 p.m.

Glossary

can a toilet; here, the large room in the dorm that houses the toilets and sinks.

Ziegfeld Follies a lavish Broadway variety show, produced by American Florenz Ziegfeld (1869–1932).

Doberman pinscher any of a breed of large dog with erect ears, a docked tail, and a short, smooth, usually dark coat with tan markings.

caddy a person who attends a golfer, carrying the clubs, finding the balls, etc.

Chapter 5

Summary

After a lackluster trip to town with Ackley and another student, Holden settles in to compose the descriptive theme paper for Stradlater. He decides to write about his brother Allie's left-handed baseball glove. Allie died of leukemia on July 18, 1946, while the family was vacationing in Maine. Holden was 13 years old at the time, Allie two years younger. Holden finishes the essay around 10:30 p.m.

Commentary

Pencey's fraudulence extends even to the menu at the dining hall. The main course on Saturday evenings is always steak. Holden suspects that the motive is to impress parents who visit on Sunday and ask their sons what they had to eat for dinner the night before.

At best, life around Agerstown is boring. Holden has no date so he takes a bus into town with Ackley and Mal Brossard, where they play pinball and eat hamburgers. They are back at the dorm by 8:45 p.m.

Literary Device

Allie's left-handed fielder's mitt (*not* a catcher's mitt, so different from Holden, who wears his hat like a catcher does—backwards) is one of the dominating symbols of the novel. It is significant because it reveals the character of Holden's cherished younger brother. Allie wrote poems, in green ink, all over the glove so that he would have something to read when he was in the field and bored. Holden tells us that Allie was extremely intelligent and the nicest member of his family. He had the kind of red hair, Holden says, that somehow told him when Allie was near, even when he couldn't see him. The night Allie died, Holden slept in the garage and broke his hand while punching out the garage windows.

Character Insight

Throughout the novel, Holden is protective of children and innocence. Surely, this is related to his feelings for Allie, whom he could not defend from death. He keeps Allie's baseball glove with him and often thinks about his brother. We might suspect that such an intimate topic will be wasted on Stradlater.

Literary Device

Chronologically, Holden was 13 when 11-year-old Allie died on July 18, 1946. He is seventeen when he tells his story. Depending on the date of Holden's birthday—and his reliability with numbers—we might make an educated guess as to the time of the action in the novel: apparently, Holden is in California, narrating the novel, sometime around the middle of 1950, probably reporting the events of late 1949.

Glossary

racket any dishonest scheme or practice.

Brown Betty a baked apple pudding made with butter, spices, sugar, and bread crumbs.

galoshes overshoes, especially high, warmly lined overshoes of rubber and fabric.

bridge any of various card games, for two pairs of players, that developed from whist.

boardwalk a walk, often made of wood and elevated, placed along a beach or seafront.

sinus any of the air cavities in the skull opening into the nasal cavities.

halitosis bad-smelling breath.

Chapters 6 and 7

Summary

The events of the rest of the evening are a little blurred in Holden's memory. Stradlater returns around 11:00 or so and reads the theme paper Holden has written, while unbuttoning his shirt and stroking his chest. Stradlater is in love with himself. Of course, he doesn't understand Holden's choice of a baseball glove for a descriptive essay and condemns it. Holden grabs the paper and tears it up.

Holden becomes increasingly agitated about Stradlater's date with Jane. Although he can't know exactly what happened, his roommate's glib comments enrage him. Stradlater taunts him, and Holden misses with a wild punch. Stradlater holds him down but lets him up. Holden calls Stradlater a moron and gets a bloody nose for his trouble. Stradlater leaves. Holden decides to spend the night in Ackley's room, can't sleep, thinks of visiting Mal Brossard but changes his mind, and decides to "get the hell out of Pencey," instead of waiting until Wednesday to leave. He plans to rent an inexpensive hotel room in New York City and stay there until Wednesday, when he can go home.

Commentary

Character
Insight

Stradlater is a superficial kid who has no hope of understanding Holden's theme or the significance of a baseball glove covered with poems. Nor could he possibly value a girl who keeps her kings in the back row, when she plays checkers, because they look nice back there. Holden has been on a double date with Ward and knows what a womanizer his roommate is. He becomes increasingly upset when he learns that Stradlater made Jane late for her curfew and spent the evening, with her, parked in the basketball coach's car. When Holden asks what happened, Stradlater is arrogant and taunting. Holden tries to fight his larger, stronger roommate, but, of course, he has no chance.

Theme

Jane is an early example of Holden's devotion to those he sees as innocent. Holden sees Jane as a sensitive, imaginative girl who transcends the cruelty of life. But Stradlater sees the girl as just another potential score. He can't even keep her name straight, mistakenly calling her "Jean." Holden can't protect Jane, whether or not she needs or wants his help, any more than he could protect his brother Allie. He is frustrated and angry that the Stradlaters of the world win so often. Fed up with Pencey Prep and all it stands for, Holden decides to leave and to stay at a hotel until he can go home on Wednesday.

Glossary

backasswards similar to the slang term *ass-backwards*, meaning, done in a way that is particularly contrary to the usual way, confusing, etc.

socks hard hits with the fist.

shadow punches sparring with an imaginary opponent, especially in training as a boxer.

Give her the time here, engage in sexual activity with the girl.

pacifist one who is opposed to the use of force under any circumstances; specifically, one who refuses for reasons of conscience to participate in war or any military action.

Canasta a card game, a variation of rummy, usually for two or four players, using a double deck of cards and four jokers.

Mass the Roman Catholic Eucharistic (communion) rite consisting of prayers and ceremonies centered on the consecration of bread and wine.

aces first-rate; expert. Here, Holden uses the term sarcastically to Ackley.

Gladstones light hand luggage with two hinged compartments.

Chapters 8 and 9

Summary

It is too late to get a taxi in Agerstown so Holden walks to the train station. He lowers the earflaps on his hunting cap to protect against the cold. En route to New York City, he is joined at Trenton by an attractive woman who turns out to be the mother of a classmate, Ernest Morrow. Holden introduces himself as Rudolf Schmidt, actually the name of the custodian at his dorm, and invents several flattering stories about the woman's son, "Old Ernie." When Mrs. Morrow asks why he's leaving school before the end of the semester, he tells her that he has to return home because he has a brain tumor and that he must have surgery.

When he arrives at New York's Penn Station, Holden considers telephoning several people but ends up calling no one. He takes a cab to the Edmont Hotel where he observes unusual happenings from the window of his shabby room. His phone call to Miss Faith Cavendish, a young lady whose sexual reputation precedes her, ends without any plans to meet.

Commentary

As he begins the train ride to New York, Holden makes one of his many observations on "phony" art and literature. This time the target is the kind of slick magazine that features stories of romance or adventure, with girls named Linda or Marcia lighting pipes for guys named David. Sometimes, he confesses, he can actually read such tripe without puking, but not tonight. He puts his hunting cap in his pocket and just sits there until a lady boards at Trenton, choosing the front seat next to his because she is carrying a large bag.

Mrs. Morrow is the mother of Ernest, whom Holden immediately recognizes as "doubtless the biggest bastard that ever went to Pencey." Ernie is the kind of jerk who enjoys snapping his soggy towel at the other boys' butts. He really likes hurting people, and Holden suspects that Ernie will continue to be a "rat" for the rest of his life. Although he despises her son, that is not what Holden tells Mrs. Morrow, who sees her son as a "sensitive" boy who perhaps takes life too seriously.

Holden has warned us that he loves to lie. He confirms that on the ride to Penn Station. First, he introduces himself to Mrs. Morrow as Rudolf Schmidt, using the name of his dorm's janitor. Then he describes her son to Mrs. Morrow in glowing, grown-up terms. Old Ernie "adapts" very well, something that anyone who has been away at school will recognize as a universal adult virtue. Her son is a complex guy, according to Holden, the sort of fellow who is a little difficult to get to know at first but only because he is an original, one of a kind. Ernie is enormously "popular," another adult virtue that most of us fail to achieve. He should have been president of the class but is so modest that he refused to accept the nomination and run for office. Holden understands how mothers love to hear good things about their sons and wonders if Mrs. Morrow will always think of Ernie as the shy fellow who refused his class' nomination, even as the despicable boy becomes a despicable man.

Critics disagree about Holden's motivation. In *The Catcher in the Rye: Innocence Under Pressure* (published by Simon & Schuster), Sanford Pinsker appreciates the humor of the encounter but sees "disguised hostility" in Holden. Is Caulfield mean-spirited here, or is he merely trying to make Mrs. Morrow feel good? We know that Holden can be cruel, as evidenced, for example, by his fascination with Ackley's physical shortcomings (his problems with acne, his round-shouldered homeliness). On the surface, Holden seems to be kind to Mrs. Morrow, telling us that he likes her. We might fast forward, however, to the conversation that soon may take place between Mrs. Morrow and Ernest. She most likely will learn that Rudolf Schmidt is the janitor, and she will know that she has been tricked by the boy she met on the train. Is Holden sufficiently aware to realize this, or is he just careless?

Because of his situation and his view of the world, Holden is lonely. When he arrives at Penn Station, he enters a phone booth to call someone but can't think of anyone he can reach out to at that time of night. (It must be well after 1:00 a.m.) He takes a cab to the Edmont Hotel but initially and, it seems, inadvertently, gives the driver his parents' address. Psychoanalytical critics jump on this as a *Freudian slip* (a mistake made in speaking, by which, it is thought, a person inadvertently reveals unconscious motives or desires) that reveals Holden's subconscious yearning for home. That may be. Or it could be just what he says it is: habit.

Literary Device

At the Edmont, Holden is assigned to a "very crumby" room with a view of nothing but the other side of the hotel. The view, however, proves somewhat interesting. In one room is a transvestite, a distinguished-looking older gentleman enjoying himself as he dons silk stockings, high heels, a bra, a corset, and a black evening dress. In another, a couple laughingly spits some kind of liquid—perhaps water or alcohol—all over each other. Although Holden decides that the hotel is filled with "perverts," he likes to watch. He is concerned about his own sexuality and confesses that he has certain yearnings but doesn't understand sex very well. Like many young people, he has made rules (apparently of limitation or abstinence) for himself but usually breaks them, sometimes soon after they are made.

Having been reminded of sex, Holden recalls that a Princeton student gave him the number of a girl in New York who reportedly is very friendly and, though not a prostitute, is casual sexually. Holden calls Miss Faith Cavendish, probably waking her up, and fails to convince her that she should see him that night. She does offer to meet him the next day, but Holden declines and ends the conversation; he immediately regrets the lost opportunity—a terribly lame attempt at intimacy.

Glossary

earlap earflap; either of a pair of cloth or fur flaps on a cap, turned down to protect the ears from cold.

lousy with rocks here, wearing a good deal of jewelry, possibly diamonds.

cocktail any of various alcoholic drinks made of a distilled liquor mixed with a wine, fruit juice, etc., and usually iced.

incognito with true identity unrevealed or disguised; under an assumed name, rank, etc.

bellboy a person employed by a hotel, club, etc. to carry luggage and do errands.

highballs tall glasses of liquor, usually whiskey or brandy, mixed with water, soda water, ginger ale, etc. and served with ice.

suave smoothly gracious or polite; polished; blandly ingratiating; urbane.

Princeton a prestigious university in Princeton, New Jersey; part of the Ivy League, a group of colleges in the northeastern United States forming a league for intercollegiate sports and other activities.

Chapter 10

Summary

Holden claims that it is still early, but it is actually quite late. However, the Lavender Room, a lounge off the lobby of the Edmont Hotel, is still open. After providing a detailed recollection of his younger sister, Phoebe, Holden visits the Lavender Room and meets three women, tourists from Seattle.

Commentary

Despite the late hour, Holden nearly calls Phoebe, his 10-year-old sister. However, he realizes that he almost certainly will have to speak to one of his parents instead.

Character Insight

Phoebe is not only intelligent and pretty, with red hair like Allie's, but she is one person with whom Holden can communicate, his soul mate. Sometimes she seems more mature than he does. Phoebe is thin like Holden; he describes her as "roller-skate skinny." She has pretty ears, and she is unusually perceptive. She knows a good movie from a lousy one, as evidenced by her adoration of the Alfred Hitchcock suspense classic *The 39 Steps* (1935). She has seen it so many times that she has memorized the dialogue.

Phoebe is a budding creative artist in her own right. She writes books featuring a girl detective named Hazle Weatherfield, an orphan who, nonetheless, has a 20-year-old father who keeps popping up. Phoebe may be Holden's best friend.

Literary Device

Holden's aesthetics are tested in the Lavender Room where the Buddy Singer band, "corny" and "putrid," holds forth. Caulfield seems to resent adults but keeps struggling to be one. He tries to order a Scotch and soda (unmixed, of course) but gets carded and settles for a Coke.

The three women in their thirties, sitting at the next table, are tourists from Seattle, all employees at the same insurance office. Holden gives them a "cool glance." Marty and Laverne are unattractive in such similar ways that Holden thinks they might be sisters, which offends both of them. Bernice is blonde, somewhat cute, and a terrific dancer, although lacking in personality. The women are concerned about Holden's age and find it amusing that he is socializing with them. He, on the other hand, can't stand their lack of taste or their touristy fascination with celebrities and Radio City Music Hall. The women excuse themselves, and Holden gets stuck with the tab.

Glossary

pimpy-looking resembling a man who is an agent for a prostitute or prostitutes and lives off their earnings.

from hunger here, unattractive, unfashionable.

grool here, an unattractive person.

Peter Lorre (1904–1964) Hungarian by birth, he was a recognizable character actor and movie star in several countries, including the United States.

Stork Club or El Morocco fashionable New York City nightclubs, where one was more likely to spot celebrities.

Tom Collins an iced drink made with gin, mixed with soda water, lime or lemon juice, and sugar; typically a summer drink.

Radio City Music Hall a Manhattan theater featuring films and stage shows, including a lavish Christmas pageant.

Chapter 11

Summary

This short chapter is devoted almost exclusively to Holden's recollections of Jane Gallagher. Sitting in a "vomity-looking" chair in the lobby of the Edmont Hotel, he remembers how they met and what they did the summer before his sophomore year. He thinks he knows her "like a book." Despite the late hour, Holden still is not tired. He decides to visit Ernie's Nightclub in Greenwich Village.

Commentary

Character
Insight

If she is as Holden remembers her, Jane is probably the one whom Holden should be dating instead of Sally Hayes. Jane lived next door to his family's summer home in Maine. Holden met her after his mother complained to the Gallaghers about their Doberman pinscher's habit of relieving itself on the Caulfield's lawn. Holden clearly appreciates and adores Jane, and she is someone he can talk with comfortably. Except for family members, she is the only person to whom he has shown Allie's baseball glove.

Holden loves Jane's idiosyncrasies. He loves it that she played golf with her eyes closed and once lost eight balls in a single round. He loves it that she is "muckle-mouthed," sending her lips in all directions when she is excited about something she is telling him. He loves it that she keeps her kings in the back row when they play checkers. He loves holding hands with her. Once, during the newsreel at the movie, she touched the back of his neck in such a way that it made a huge impression on Holden.

Character
Insight

Jane does have a problem at home, however, and it may be beyond Holden's capacity to understand completely. He notices that her alcoholic stepfather attempts to dominate her, and when Holden asks Jane what the problem is, she starts to cry. When Holden sits by her and tries to comfort her, she sobs. He kisses her all over her face, but he wants us to know that she wouldn't let him kiss her on the mouth; they weren't really "necking." Jane is very young but has a terrific figure, and

Holden wonders if maybe her stepfather has tried to "get wise" with her, but she says that the man has not. It's unlikely that Jane would admit this kind of event to Holden, and he prefers to think of her as living in innocence, untouched by the seamier side of life.

Even the hookers have left the lobby, and Holden wants to get out of the hotel for a while. He catches a cab and heads for Ernie's, a nightclub in Greenwich Village.

Glossary

glider a porch seat suspended in a frame so that it can glide or swing back and forth.

get wise with her here, to approach her sexually.

necking kissing, hugging, and caressing passionately.

Chapter 12

Summary

On the way to Ernie's, Holden discusses ducks, fish, and winter with the cab driver. At the club, Holden expresses his opinions concerning the aesthetics of performance, Ernie, the crowd in general, and a nearby couple in particular. Lillian Simmons, a former girlfriend of D.B., pops by his table with her date, a Navy officer. Holden declines her invitation to join them, saying he was just leaving.

Commentary

Character Insight

The cab driver's name is Horwitz. He is a grouchy, somewhat twisted amateur zoologist, but at least he is willing to entertain Holden's inquiry about where the ducks in Central Park go in winter. Actually, Horwitz prefers to discuss the fish. He gruffly declares that the fish have a tougher time than the ducks. Fish spend the winter frozen in the ice, according to Horwitz. They take in nourishment through the pores in their bodies. His opinions are amusing, but the comic aspects of the scene depend more on the nature of the dialogue. Holden and Horwitz sound like two old antagonists who have had this discussion a hundred times before and jump on each other's lines as ancient acquaintances do when excited about a controversial topic. Salinger beautifully captures the crisp, tough conversational sounds of the city through this dialogue.

Literary Device

Holden's aesthetics are tested at the nightclub. Despite the very late hour, Ernie's is packed, mostly with students on Christmas break. Ernie is an extremely skillful piano player, but Holden thinks that he has become too slick. Ernie has a huge mirror in front of him and a spotlight on his face so that the crowd won't miss an expression. In a way, Ernie is like Holden's brother, D.B. They both once were true artists, in Holden's mind, but have sold out: Ernie to the sycophantic fans and D.B. to Hollywood. Perhaps reflecting Salinger's values, Holden feels that an artist should live only for his art, eschewing fans and fame. When he starts pandering to the crowd, showing off with high ripples on the keys as Ernie does, he has lost his way. This crowd, of course, loves it; as Holden observes, people applaud for the wrong reasons. Ernie concludes with a "very phony, *humble* bow."

Theme

At a nearby table, some "Yale-looking guy" is talking to his date about an attempted suicide while copping a feel under the table. Several critics have noticed the juxtaposition of sex and death in the novel, this scene at Ernie's being one of the more bizarre examples. Holden concludes that he is "surrounded by jerks."

Lillian Simmons, who used to date D.B., comes by Holden's table with her date, a Navy officer. She is annoying in a bubbly, phony way that Holden finds particularly irritating. The only real thing about her may be her "very big knockers." She loves to be noticed. Holden knows that she only wants to impress him so that he will tell D.B. about her, and he quickly declines her invitation to join Lillian and her date at their table. Having told her that he was just leaving, he heads back to the hotel.

Glossary

flitty here, Holden uses the term to refer to male homosexuals.

Tattersall having a checkered pattern of dark lines on a light background.

Chapter 13

Summary

Holden is tired of taxis and walks the forty-one blocks back to the hotel, wearing his red hunting cap with the earflaps down, missing his pilfered gloves, and bemoaning his cowardice. The elevator man, Maurice, doubles as a pimp and offers to provide Holden with female companionship for "five bucks a throw" or fifteen dollars for the night. Holden agrees to go for "a throw" in his room, 1222, but almost immediately regrets it. The hooker calls herself Sunny; Holden tells her his name is Jim Steele. Although they do little more than talk, because Holden is more depressed than ready to have sex, Sunny says that her fee is ten dollars. Holden pays her only five, and she leaves, calling him a "crumb-bum."

Commentary

Holden's reflection on his cowardice and inept fighting ability foreshadows events in the next chapter. He realizes that he is more likely to attack someone verbally. What frightens him most in such a conflict is having to look at the other fellow's face.

As he waits for the prostitute, Holden passes time by brushing his teeth and changing his shirt. He confesses to being "a little nervous" and admits that he is still a virgin. The truth is that Holden, at age 16, seems to be what we might call a "good kid." When he is making out with a girl and she asks him to stop, he stops. "No" means no for Holden. He is interested in sex, but he doesn't quite understand how to get there.

What he learns with Sunny is that he prefers not to get there with a prostitute. The whole scene is depressing rather than erotic for Holden. He has to get to know a girl, and like her a lot, before he is comfortable with intimacy. One of the likable things about Holden is that, beneath it all, he has some healthy values. In addition, he has mixed feelings toward Sunny. She is very young (about Holden's age) and seems to be almost as nervous as he is. As Holden describes it, "She crossed her legs and started jiggling this one foot up and down. She was very nervous, for a prostitute. She really was. I think it was because she was young as hell. She was around my age." Holden is depressed that she is so young leading this kind of life. It saddens him to think of her going to a store to buy the green dress that she has worn for him and that he hangs in the closet so it won't get "all wrinkly," as Sunny puts it, in her child-like language. When "Jim Steele" says he is 22, she responds, "Like fun you are." And yet, there is something very spooky about Sunny. Holden tells us that this child with her squeaky little voice is much more frightening than a "big old prostitute, with a lot of makeup on her face and all. . . ."

Literary Device

The names, "Sunny" and "Jim Steele," are ironic; neither name fits the person. Freudian critics delight in analyzing their significance. Remember that Salinger's boyhood nickname was "Sonny." What kind of Freudian slip has Salinger made by naming the prostitute "Sunny"? What has he revealed about himself? "Steele," some critics suggest, is a strained attempt at phallic superiority.

Style & Language

Holden needs a way out of this "big mess." He promptly decides that an elaborate lie is best. He claims that he recently had surgery on his "clavichord," which Holden may or may not know is an old musical keyboard instrument. He tells Sunny that the clavichord is located "quite a ways down in the spinal canal." Sunny's response is to come on stronger. She sits on his lap and says he is cute. She says he reminds her of some guy in the movies. Then she starts talking crudely, and Holden ends the session. Sunny says her fee is ten dollars, but Holden insists on paying her only the five that Maurice mentioned. He fetches her dress from the closet, and she leaves. Sunny again reminds us of a child as her parting curse is to call Holden a "crumb-bum."

Glossary

yellow cowardly.

rake an immoral, corrupt, depraved man.

polo coat a loose-fitting overcoat made of camel's hair or some such fabric.

nonchalant showing cool lack of concern; casually indifferent.

Chapter 14

Summary

It is dawn on Sunday by the time that Sunny exits. Holden smokes a couple of cigarettes and reflects on his relationship with his deceased brother, Allie, as well as his feelings about religion. He is summoned by a knock on the door. Sunny has returned with Maurice and demands the rest of the ten dollars. Holden resists and is roughed up by the pimp.

Commentary

Literary
Device

Although Allie does not appear as a character in the novel, he is a significant presence. When Holden gets very depressed, he sometimes talks "sort of out loud" to his younger brother. He does so after Sunny leaves. His communication with Allie is almost religious, a confession of Holden's boyhood lack of consideration for the kid. In the hotel room, Holden repeatedly tells Allie, out loud, to get his bike and join him at the home of a childhood friend, Bobby Fallon. Holden once refused to take Allie with him when he and Bobby were going shooting with BB guns, and the guilt he feels about this incident prompts him to repeat those words, almost in an attempt to take back that day and do it differently.

Character
Insight

In bed, Holden has greater difficulty with conventional prayer. He wants to speak with Jesus but can't. He "likes" Jesus but finds the Disciples annoying and considers himself an atheist. He is bothered that the Disciples repeatedly let Jesus down, indicating the importance of friendship and loyalty to Holden.

Literary
Device

It is telling that, other than Jesus, Holden's favorite character in the Bible is "that lunatic and all, that lived in the tombs and kept cutting himself with stones." He refers to Mark 5: 1–20, in which Jesus meets the troubled soul whose "name is Legion: for we are many." Holden himself is a troubled soul and, like the man from the tombs, resists being tamed. Recall that he tells us his story from a mental health clinic or sanitarium in California. It is little wonder that Holden identifies with the madman. Holden, too, is one of the legion, one of the many.

Sunny and Maurice interrupt Holden's spiritual musings. They want the other five dollars they say Holden owes them. Holden struggles but is no match for the bigger, stronger, meaner Maurice. As if he has learned nothing from his fight with Stradlater, Holden also calls Maurice a "moron" and is doubled over by a blow to the belly. Sunny takes the five dollars from Holden's wallet, and she and Maurice leave with the money. Holden vamps into a tough guy fantasy in which he has been shot and seeks revenge. He doesn't really feel very tough though. Instead, he feels like committing suicide.

Glossary

Quaker a member of the Society of Friends, a Christian denomination founded in England (circa 1650) by George Fox; the Friends have no formal creed, rites, liturgy, or priesthood, and reject violence in human relations, including war. The term "Quaker" was originally derisive, aimed at the Friends because of Fox's admonition to "quake" at the word of the Lord.

Judas Judas Iscariot, the disciple who betrayed Jesus (Matthew 26:14, 48).

chisel to take advantage of by cheating.

rubbernecks people who stretch their necks or turn their heads to gaze about in curiosity.

Chapter 15

Summary

Holden awakes around 10:00 Sunday morning. He phones an old girlfriend, Sally Hayes, and makes a date to meet her at 2:00 p.m. to catch a theater matinee. Holden checks out of the hotel and leaves his bags at a lock box in Grand Central Station. While eating a large breakfast (orange juice, bacon and eggs, toast and coffee) at a sandwich bar, he meets two nuns who are schoolteachers from Chicago, newly assigned to a convent "way the hell uptown," apparently near Washington Heights. They discuss *Romeo and Juliet*, and Holden gives them a donation of ten dollars.

Commentary

Character Insight

Holden is confused about women, and that shows in his relationship with Sally Hayes. Sally is everything that Jane Gallagher is not: conventional, superficial, stupid, and phony. She knows about theater and literature, and for a while that fooled Holden into thinking she was intelligent. But she uses words like "grand,"—as in, "I'd love to. Grand."—and annoys with her pretense. Briefly, Holden wishes he had not called her. However, Sally is someone to spend the day with, and she *is* very good-looking. Holden is both drawn to and repelled by her. At least he knows what to expect.

Theme

Holden dislikes the theater almost as much as the movies. Both are contrived and artificial, and the audiences applaud for the wrong reasons, just as they did at Ernie's. The meeting with the nuns further reveals Holden's aesthetics, his sense of taste in the arts. Because one of the nuns is an English teacher, they begin to discuss Shakespeare's tragedy *Romeo and Juliet*. It is no surprise that Holden's favorite character is Mercutio, Romeo's glib, subversive best friend. Holden resents betrayal, even accidental betrayal, and he dislikes Romeo after the hero inadvertently causes Tybalt to kill Mercutio. Mercutio is Holden's kind of guy: bright and fun, a bit of a smart-mouth. Holden finds the drama "quite moving," but we suspect that he would have preferred a play in which Mercutio is the main character.

Character Insight

Holden feels good about the donation he has given to the nuns, but he is becoming concerned about money. He left Pencey with quite a "wad of dough" because his grandmother had just sent him a lavish birthday gift. (She has a faulty memory and sends him birthday money several times a year.) But Holden is careless with money. What he doesn't spend, he loses. He rather foolishly paid for all of the drinks for the tourist girls at the Lavender Room, and he dropped ten bucks (a considerable amount of money in 1949) on Sunny. Now he faces a date with Sally who, we might suspect, is not low-maintenance.

Glossary

necked kissed, hugged, and caressed passionately.

matinee a reception or performance, as of a play, held in the afternoon.

West Point military reservation in southeastern New York state; site of the U.S. Military Academy.

Grand Central Station a famous, expansive train station in New York City.

bourgeois of or characteristic of a person whose beliefs, attitudes, and practices are conventionally middle-class.

Chapter 16

Summary

When Holden finishes his conversation with the two nuns, it is almost noon. He has two hours until he is to meet Sally at the Biltmore Hotel so he goes for a walk toward Broadway. He wants to buy a recording, for Phoebe, of an old song called "Little Shirley Beans." Along the way, Holden notices an apparently underprivileged family walking home from church. The young son is walking in the street and singing.

Fortunately, the first music store that he visits has a copy of the record. Holden tries to telephone Jane, but her mother answers so he hangs up. Still burdened with the responsibility of procuring theater tickets, he chooses a play, *I Know My Love*, that he thinks Sally will like because it stars the Lunts. He decides to visit Central Park in hopes of finding Phoebe who often skates there on Sundays. He almost visits the Museum of Natural History but decides not to go in. Although he doesn't feel like going through with the date, he catches a cab to meet Sally at the Biltmore Hotel as planned.

Commentary

Theme

Much of the chapter is devoted to Holden's considerations of artistic performances. Simply put, he likes what he finds to be authentic and dislikes what he sees as phony. The dominating theme of the rest of the chapter is the mutability of time and its relationship to death.

Literary Device

The first example of Holden's aesthetics in Chapter 16 is the recording that he wants to buy for Phoebe, an old song about a shy kid who won't go out of her house because she is missing two front teeth. It is called "Little Shirley Beans" and is sung by the black jazz singer Estelle Fletcher. What Holden likes is that it is authentic. Despite the topic, it is neither maudlin nor sentimental. The artist sings it "very Dixieland and whorehouse," not all mushy and *cute* the way he thinks a white girl would do it. Holden consistently holds in contempt any artist who caters to the audience at the expense of the work of art, even a song about a girl missing two front teeth. He feels the same way about

Ernie's piano playing or D.B.'s writing. Holden pays five dollars for the recording at a time when most records could be purchased for fifty cents or less.

Theme

A less professional example of authenticity is the kid on the street. He is "swell" because he goes his own way. The parents are on the sidewalk, but the kid marches along the street, next to the curb, singing, "If a body catch a body coming through the rye." He has a pretty voice and is just singing "for the hell of it." Cars zoom by, some apparently having to screech their brakes to miss the boy, but he is not perturbed. For Holden, this is pure, innocent, and real, a living example of art for art's sake although he does not state it that way. The performance is the better because neither the kid nor Holden, his only audience, takes it very seriously. The event brightens Holden's day. The scene is even more significant because it foreshadows Salinger's revelation of the central metaphor of the novel, the source of the novel's title, in Chapter 22.

In contrast are movies and the theater. It "depresses hell" out of Holden when people make too much of going to a movie, especially when they form lines all the way down the block. Live performances are just as bad. He hates Broadway, and he hates actors, even the so-called "great" performers like Sir Laurence Olivier. When D.B. took Phoebe and Holden to see Olivier's legendary performance in Shakespeare's *Hamlet*, Holden didn't much care for it. He thought that Olivier was handsome and had a great voice but acted more like a general than a "sad, screwed-up" guy struggling to find his way, which is what he thought the play was supposed to be about. Holden usually does not enjoy performances because he is concerned that the actors will do something phony at almost any moment. Even if an actor is good, Holden thinks the actor acts as though he *knows* he's good and ends up pandering to the audience the way Ernie does when he plays the piano. Audiences usually can't distinguish between phony and authentic, as Holden sees it, and applaud at all the wrong times.

Theme

The chapter's other major theme is the mutability of time and its relationship to death. At the park, Holden runs into a schoolmate of Phoebe's who suggests that Holden's sister might be at the museum, "the one with the Indians." That proves to be unlikely, since it is Sunday and Phoebe's class would not be meeting, but mention of the Museum of Natural History triggers memories for Holden. He attended Phoebe's school when he was her age and toured the same museum. He likes to think that the museum would be pretty much the same if he visits it now, but it bothers him to think that *he* has changed. Phoebe, too, will change. Life *is* change, as most of us learn, but Holden doesn't want to accept that. He likes the glass cases in the museum that freeze a moment of history in time and space. An Eskimo, for example, might be fishing through a hole in the ice. The same Eskimo was there when Holden visited the museum and will be there for Phoebe when she visits. Holden would like it if our lives, too, could be frozen in time. It is an adolescent view of the world, the motive behind a young person's saying to a friend, "Don't ever change." The wish is impossible, but it is shared by Holden. He'd surely like to freeze certain moments with Allie or Phoebe for all time: "Certain things they should stay the way they are. You ought to be able to stick them in one of those big glass cases and just leave them alone." In Holden's world, good things would never die.

Glossary

Broadway street running north and south through New York City, known as the center of the city's main theater and entertainment section.

the Lunts Alfred Lunt (1893–1977) and Lynn Fontanne (1887–1983), husband and wife, were revered stage actors of the day, often performing together.

Flys Up a baseball or softball playground game in which the fielder who catches a fly ball is allowed to bat next.

Chapter 17

Summary

Sally is ten minutes late but looks terrific in her black coat and matching beret. She is thrilled that they will get to see the Lunts and is impressed by the performance. Holden is less than thrilled, first by the performance on stage and then by Sally's performance in the lobby. He dislikes the way she talks with an Andover student named George. After the show, they go ice skating at Radio City. Holden tries to talk with Sally about things of real importance to Holden. He asks her to run off to Massachusetts and Vermont with him. The date ends badly, and he walks out.

Commentary

Theme

The dominating theme of Chapter 17 is compatibility, or lack of it, between couples. The opening scene, the play, and the exchange at the skating rink all deal with the question of life partners and what a disaster it is to have the wrong one.

Style & Language

The question first occurs to Holden as he waits for Sally under the clock at the Biltmore Hotel. He is girl watching in his own way. Instead of wondering what it would be like to be with this girl or that, temporarily, Holden's mind drifts. He begins to wonder what will "*happen* to all of them." What kinds of life partners—"dopey guys," as he calls them—will they find? Some probably will end up with petulant jerks who pout if they lose a game of golf. Others will marry mean guys or boring guys or guys who never read a book. Typically, Holden then digresses about a boring guy he knew who could whistle exceptionally well. Considering the events about to unfold, perhaps he should worry more about the kind of partner he may end up with. Sally is convenient and familiar and available, but she is no Jane Gallagher.

The theater play tells the story of two life partners from youth to old age. The partners seem compatible but artificial. Holden thinks the show is "on the crappy side," but he concedes that the Lunts are pretty good. However, he concludes that they are *too* good, like Ernie at his piano, and that they show off for the audience. The play's storyline takes the couple through various trials of life, and Holden concedes that it is not the worst he has seen.

From the beginning, Sally seems like an odd match for Holden. She is extremely phony. Everything is "marvelous" or "lovely" for Sally, but we get the idea that she doesn't really *feel* things the way Holden does. At the intermission, she is mostly concerned with seeing and being seen. Finally she spots George, from Andover, whom, Holden suspects, she probably has met only once. She greets him like a life-long friend. He is a fellow phony, saying that the Lunts are "absolute angels," and he is even Sally's match at name-dropping. Sally and George should ride off together into the future, cocktails at the club in hand.

At the skating rink, Holden makes the mistake of trying to talk with Sally about his passions. But he only confuses and frightens her. She asks him not to shout and says she has no idea what he is talking about. Instead of backing off, Holden soars. He suggests that they borrow a car and take off for a couple of weeks to Massachusetts and Vermont. They could get a cabin. It's beautiful up there. Maybe they could get married and live there forever.

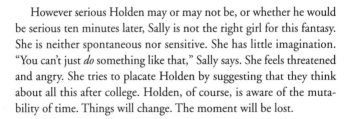

However serious Holden may or may not be, or whether he would be serious ten minutes later, Sally is not the right girl for this fantasy. She is neither spontaneous nor sensitive. She has little imagination. "You can't just *do* something like that," Sally says. She feels threatened and angry. She tries to placate Holden by suggesting that they think about all this after college. Holden, of course, is aware of the muta-bility of time. Things will change. The moment will be lost.

The disagreement turns angry, and Holden tells Sally that she gives him "a royal pain in the ass." Suffice to say that, after this remark, the date is over. Sally says she will get home on her own. Holden leaves her at the skating rink bar.

It finally occurs to Holden that maybe Sally was not the right girl to ask about such a venture. He is right. Sally is a practical girl, ambi-tious in conventional ways, greedy, a bit of a social climber, who will get what she wants when she wants it, because she always *has*. We can be sure that, throughout life, Sally will never be caught leaving her kings in the back row.

Glossary

bunk talk that is empty, insincere, or merely for effect.

rubbering short for *rubbernecking*, meaning to look at things or gaze about in curiosity.

cliques small, exclusive circles of people; snobbish or narrow circles of friends who share a common interest or background.

fantastic here, existing in the imagination; imaginary; unreal.

Chapters 18 and 19

Summary

It is late afternoon or very early evening on Sunday. Holden telephones Carl Luce, whom he knew during his days at the Whooton School. Carl is three years older and was his student adviser. They agree to meet for a drink at the Wicker Bar in the Seton Hotel at 10:00 p.m. With time to kill, and since he is there already, he attends a stage show and movie at Radio City Music Hall. He sees the Rockettes, the Christmas pageant, and a war film. At the bar, Holden manages to get served, this time, even though he is underage. When Luce arrives, he reveals that he is dating an older woman, a Chinese sculptress in her late thirties who lives in Greenwich Village. He leaves for a date after having one drink with Holden.

Commentary

Literary
Device

These relatively insignificant chapters chronicle the beginning of Holden's slow descent into a hellish night. It is no surprise that he resents the artificiality of the stage show at Radio City or finds the war movie "putrid." The only wonder is that he attends at all.

On his way to the bar, Holden's reflections on the film lead to some further considerations of literature. He dislikes Ernest Hemingway's novel *A Farewell to Arms* (1929), apparently thinking of it as a war story and, of course, "phony"; but he appreciates F. Scott Fitzgerald's *The Great Gatsby* (1925) and an unnamed work by Ring Lardner.

Character
Insight

For a fellow who dislikes phonies so much, Holden collects more than his share; Luce is an obvious example. At the age of 19, he poses as a worldly sophisticate. Holden is slightly suspicious but impressed nonetheless. At Whooton, Luce presented himself to the younger boys as an expert on sex, his specialty supposedly being "perverts." Holden was, and still is, confused about the subject of sex, but he is very interested in Luce's insights. Luce's alleged Shanghai girlfriend, in her late thirties, fascinates Holden. He thinks maybe he should move to China and get in on some of the "philosophy" that Luce espouses. Then he wonders if he should pursue psychoanalysis, because Luce, whose father is a psychoanalyst, speaks well of it.

Character Insight

The sad truth is that Holden does not know which way to turn, and he will spend the rest of the night demonstrating it. He is intrigued by anyone who seems to have a handle on life. His own sexuality bothers him, as he openly admits in the conversation with Luce. Holden thinks he has a problem because he has to like a girl a lot in order to be intimate with her. If Luce were nearly as mature, or perceptive, as he likes to pretend, he would simply tell Holden that the slightly younger man's feelings are admirable.

Glossary

Lastex trademarked term for a fine, round, rubber thread wound with cotton, rayon, silk, etc., and woven or knitted into fabric.

half gainer a fancy dive in which the diver springs from the board facing forward and does a back flip in the air so as to enter the water headfirst, facing the board.

inferiority complex any feeling of inferiority, inadequacy, etc.; originally a psychiatric term.

Rockettes dancers at New York City's Radio City Music Hall, known for their chorus-line precision.

Charles Dickens (1812–1870) English novelist.

Great Dane any of a breed of very large, muscular dog with pointed, erect ears, a square muzzle, and a short, thick, smooth coat.

furlough a leave of absence granted to military enlisted personnel for a specified period.

Ring Lardner (1885–1933) U.S. sports reporter and humorist.

louse a person regarded as mean, contemptible, etc.

snowing deceiving, misleading, or winning over by glib talk, flattery, etc.

goose to prod suddenly and playfully in the backside so as to startle.

Chapter 20

Summary

Holden stays at the bar and gets quite drunk. He decides to telephone Jane Gallagher but calls Sally Hayes instead. She tells him to go home and go to bed. Holden strikes up a conversation with the piano player. He tells Holden to go home and go to bed. Holden asks the hatcheck girl for a date. She tells him to go home and go to bed. Ignoring the unanimous advice, Holden heads for Central Park to look for the ducks. The search is in vain, and he manages to break Phoebe's record in the process. Holden reflects on Allie's funeral, which he could not attend because he was in the hospital with his broken hand (and possibly for emotional evaluation). His memory of Allie's grave at the cemetery depresses him. Finally, he decides to sneak home and visit Phoebe in case he dies, too.

Commentary

Style & Language

From time to time throughout the novel, Holden has Jane on his mind. He wants to reach out to her but decides not to or fails in his attempt. In one of his better moves, he decides he is too drunk to call Jane. But Sally is a different matter. Despite the late hour, and the fact that her grandmother says Sally is asleep, she comes to the phone. Holden tells her, "Rocky's mob got me." In his mind, he is playing gangsters again. Under the circumstances, Sally is remarkably understanding and even suggests that he call her the next day.

Literary Device

Holden's confused quest continues. At the park, he has a difficult time finding the lagoon. When he does, there are no ducks. Wherever the ducks go during winter, they apparently have gone. Holden is cold, drunk, and alone. Now he notices that he is also nearly broke. He has three ones, five quarters, and a nickel with him. With the wisdom of the inebriated, he decides to skip the coins across the part of the lagoon that is not frozen.

Holden's memories of Allie continue to haunt him. It wouldn't be so bad if Allie weren't in that "crazy cemetery" surrounded by tombstones and dead people. Holden wonders about his own mortality, which is a major part of his obsession with Allie's death. He wonders whether he is getting pneumonia and speculates on his family's reaction to his tragic passing. It would be especially hard on Phoebe, he concludes, so he leaves the park to see her.

Glossary

halitosis bad-smelling breath.

Chapter 21

Summary

Holden wants to visit Phoebe at the family apartment, in the middle of the night, without his parents' knowledge. Fortunately, there is a new elevator operator on duty who does not recognize him. Holden pretends to be visiting the Dicksteins who have an apartment on the same floor as his parents. Using his key to enter, Holden sneaks to Phoebe's room only to realize that she now is sleeping in D.B.'s room because he is away in Hollywood; she likes the huge desk and bed. Holden peruses items on her desk, by lamplight, until he wakens Phoebe. She reveals that their parents are out for the evening and will return very late. The maid is in the apartment to care for the girl. As they talk, Phoebe guesses that Holden has been expelled and concludes that their father will kill him. Upset, she hides her head under a pillow. Holden goes to the living room for cigarettes.

Commentary

Character Insight

Phoebe's significance in the novel is crucial. Despite her youth, she sometimes seems to be Holden's best friend. He can confide in her and share his dreams. Like a real friend, she does not always agree. She often sees right through her brother, detecting early on that he has been kicked out of Pencey Prep. Her advice frequently is superior to what Holden plans to do. Phoebe is also Holden's most trusted connection to family and home. On the other hand, she has trouble understanding Holden's darker side. She wonders why he is so self-destructive and why he doesn't just succeed in school the way she does. She may not quite grasp what he means by being the "catcher in the rye."

Phoebe is also a fascinating character in her own right. One way that Salinger shows this is through the indirect device of Holden's examination of all the "stuff" on her desk. In her arithmetic book, Phoebe has written her name as "Phoebe Weatherfield Caulfield." Her actual middle name is Josephine, but Holden tells us that she hates it and is always trying others on for size. In this case, she has chosen the last name of her own fictional girl detective, Hazle Weatherfield. Phoebe shares with her brother a desire to make life a little more interesting.

We learn that Phoebe is a good student but she is best in spelling. What she really seems best at, though, is being Phoebe. Her notebooks reveal a 10-year-old with a rich imagination, deep secrets to share with friends, and a healthy curiosity about her own identity. Although she wonders who she is, she clearly is not *lost* as Holden is. Holden finds stability in his younger sister.

Some of Phoebe's charm derives from the fact that she is only 10 years old, and Holden (like Salinger) values the innocence and authenticity of childhood. She is passionate about sharing a special movie with her best friend, Alice. Elephants "knock her out," and she wears blue pajamas with red elephants on the collars. A leading role (as Benedict Arnold) in the school play thrills her; she insists that Holden must attend Friday night's performance. Phoebe shares Holden's tendency toward digression, to the point that he has to interrupt her three times to discover when their parents are scheduled to return.

Phoebe is also a compassionate person, a girl with a heart. When Holden shows her the smashed recording of "Little Shirley Beans," Phoebe instantly senses the importance of the gift and wants to save the pieces, which she sticks in the drawer of her nightstand. She seems considerably more concerned about Holden's dismissal from Pencey than he is.

Glossary

foyer an entrance hall of a house or apartment.

sagitarius Phoebe, whose best subject is spelling, has misspelled "Sagittarius," the ninth sign of the zodiac, entered by the sun about November 21.

taurus Taurus (capital "T") is the second sign of the zodiac, entered by the sun about April 21.

Benedict Arnold 1741–1801) notorious American Revolutionary War general, who became a traitor and attempted to surrender West Point to the British.

Annapolis the capital of Maryland and location of the United States Naval Academy.

windbreaker a warm jacket of leather, wool, etc., having a closefitting elastic waistband and cuffs.

Chapter 22

Summary

Phoebe continues to be terribly upset over Holden's dismissal from Pencey Prep. She is sure that their father will be very upset with her brother. Holden says he'll merely be sent to a military school, *if* he is still around; he plans to head for Colorado to work on a ranch. Holden tries to explain to Phoebe what a terrible place Pencey is. He doesn't like anything there. But she concludes that he doesn't like anything *anywhere* and challenges him to name one thing that he likes. Holden tries to focus on the issue, but his mind drifts. Phoebe interrupts and repeats the challenge to think of one thing that Holden likes. He says he likes Allie, but Phoebe counters that Allie is dead and doesn't count. He says he likes talking with *her*, but Phoebe answers, "That isn't anything *really*." Phoebe changes the topic and asks Holden to name something he would like to *be*. After some consideration, he says he would like to be the catcher in the rye and explains to her what that means to him.

Commentary

Theme

In this crucial chapter, Salinger uses Phoebe's concern to elicit, from Holden, the dominating metaphor of the novel as well as its title. He sets this up with the tragic, moving story of a courageous innocent, James Castle.

Literary Device

Holden is confused throughout the novel. His thoughts drift. He tends to digress. Some of the most effective parts of the novel are Holden's digressions. An excellent example is the James Castle memory. Castle was a skinny, quiet, weak-looking schoolmate of Holden's at Elkton Hills. He had amazing resolve. One day, James voiced an opinion that an arrogant ruffian named Phil Stabile was "conceited," which he was. When word got back to Stabile, he and several cohorts locked Castle in his room and did unspeakable things to him, trying to get James to take back his comment, but James refused. To escape, he jumped out the window to his death. At the time of his death, Castle was wearing a turtleneck sweater that Holden had loaned him for a planned outing with a visitor.

The significance of James Castle's brave though ill-considered and tragic death is that it strikes home, once more, Holden's concern about protecting innocence. Holden says that he hardly knew James, but he feels an apparent closeness, perhaps symbolized by the fact that Castle died in Holden's sweater. Holden mentions that the two were linked alphabetically at roll call: "Cabel, R., Cabel, W., Castle, Caulfield." We can imagine the sensitive Holden's reaction the first time the roll was called without James' name. Some critics want to make something more of Castle's martyrdom, noting that he shares initials with another classic martyr, Jesus Christ, although that seems a stretch. It's enough that life's cruel side took another innocent victim, and Holden would like to do what he can to stop that.

When Phoebe asks Holden what he would like to *be*, she first suggests traditional professions such as a scientist or a lawyer. Holden quickly rejects those. Because it is Phoebe, he feels comfortable revealing an inner truth. What he'd really like to be is "the catcher in the rye." Holden misunderstands the line from the Robert Burns lyric that he heard the boy singing in Chapter 16. Holden thinks that the line is, "If a body catch a body comin' through the rye." Phoebe corrects him. The actual line, she says, is, "If a body *meet* a body coming through the rye."

Holden has a vision of thousands of small children playing in a field of rye. A cliff borders the field. In their abandon, the innocent children symbolically run too close to the edge and may fall. Holden would be there to catch them. He would be the catcher in the rye.

Phoebe doesn't respond for a long time. Then she says, with all practicality, "Daddy's going to kill you." Although she may be Holden's best friend, Phoebe occasionally demonstrates that she is only 10 years old and unable to understand the depth of Holden's desire.

Holden wants to call Mr. Antolini, his former teacher at Elkton Hills. Now an English instructor at New York University, Antolini and his wife might allow Holden to stay with them. Phoebe undercuts the intensity of the moment. Like a kid, she quickly has moved past the catcher in the rye. She casually reports that her friend Phyllis has been giving her belching lessons while Holden was at Pencey, and Phoebe demonstrates what she has learned.

Glossary

ostracizing banishing, barring, excluding, etc., from a group or from acceptance by society.

fraternity a group of male students joined together by common interests, for fellowship, etc.

cockeyed tilted to one side; crooked, awry.

Robert Burns (1759–1796) Scottish poet.

rye a hardy cereal grass, widely grown for its grain and straw.

Chapter 23

Summary

On the telephone, Mr. Antolini tells Holden to come right over if he wants. Holden returns to D.B.'s room, now inhabited by Phoebe. She has the radio on, and they dance. Holden lights a cigarette, and Phoebe explains how she can fake a fever.

Suddenly, they hear their parents entering the apartment. Holden turns out the lamp, jams out the cigarette, and hides in the closet. His mother checks on Phoebe and, smelling the cigarette, scolds her for smoking. After the mother leaves, Phoebe loans Holden her Christmas money, which makes Holden cry. He gives her his treasured red hunting cap and exits down the building's back stairs.

Commentary

This chapter is primarily a transitional one, serving to wrap up the visit and get Holden out of the apartment. Salinger offers a little insight into Mr. Antolini's character, detailing his compassionate response to the death of James Castle and his excellence as a teacher. In addition, we learn a little more about Phoebe and why Holden cherishes her.

Phoebe is delightfully serious at times. Holden has taught her the basics of dancing, and she is proud that she has been practicing and improving. She can even tango. She dances four numbers with Holden. In between songs, she stands perfectly still, not even speaking, waiting for the music to resume. She is also seriously proud of a new accomplishment, learning to fake a fever. Her friend Alice taught her the procedure: "cross your legs and hold your breath and think of something very, very hot." She assures Holden that when he tests her forehead, she won't burn his hand, she won't abuse her powers.

Because he is nearly broke, Holden asks if he might borrow some money from Phoebe. He is moved to tears when his sister gives him her Christmas stash, eight dollars and sixty-five cents. Holden's emotions frighten Phoebe, but they are not surprising. He is not nearly as independent as he pretends to be. In addition, physically and mentally, he is barely maintaining a delicate balance between function and collapse. Leaving the apartment, he is somewhat careless about making noise. He tells us that he almost wishes that his parents would catch him. Holden is 16 years old, confused, depressed, and lonely. It's almost Christmas. He needs a home.

Glossary

dough money.

Chapter 24

Summary

It is very late when Holden arrives at the Antolinis' "swanky" apartment on Sutton Place. The couple hosted a party earlier in the evening, and Mr. Antolini is still drinking heavily. Mrs. Antolini (Lillian) makes coffee and goes to bed. Holden feels dizzy and has a headache. The coffee does not help Holden. Mr. Antolini ignores his coffee and fixes himself another highball. Holden discusses an Oral Expression course, taught by Mr. Vinson at Pencey, which Holden failed. Antolini defends the instructor.

Mr. Antolini is about the same age as Holden's brother, D.B., and usually seems like a great guy. Tonight he wants to discuss pedagogy more than Holden cares to. He also offers long-winded theories concerning Holden that the boy could do without. Holden is very tired. He has slept only two or three hours since Saturday morning, two days ago. It has been an exhausting weekend. He and Antolini make up the couch, and Holden falls asleep.

Suddenly, Holden is awakened. He is shocked to find Antolini sitting on the floor by the couch, patting Holden's head. Holden becomes very upset and insists on leaving. He decides that Mr. Antolini is a pervert.

Commentary

Character Insight

Holden becomes increasingly disillusioned with Mr. Antolini. He initially tells us that the instructor was the best teacher he has ever known. Antolini is a kind of mentor, almost an older brother. Holden compares him to D.B., whom he clearly admires despite his brother's relocation to Hollywood. Young, articulate, and popular, Antolini is also intensely caring as evidenced by his continuing concern for Holden as well as his attentions to the mangled body of James Castle. But in this chapter, Holden discovers the feet of clay on his golden idol. Whether Holden's ultimate judgment (that Antolini is "perverty") is accurate or not, he is forced to recognize that Antolini does have his problems.

Holden already knows that Antolini is a heavy drinker. When the teacher greets him at the door with a highball in hand, Holden passes it off as "sophisticated." Nonetheless, the excessive drinking does bother Holden. He mentions it several times and notices that, when coffee is served, Mr. Antolini just fixes himself another highball. Holden thinks that Antolini should be careful or he "may get to be an alcoholic."

Well on his way to drunkenness, Antolini shows a side of himself that is especially annoying to Holden. Sounding very much like old Mr. Spencer at Pencey Prep, the instructor pontificates on pedagogy, specifically defending the teaching techniques of Mr. Vinson, who offers a class called "Oral Expression" at Pencey. Holden flunked the course but dislikes Vinson more because the man is cruel and shallow. If a student gives a speech and strays from the point, Vinson insists that the other boys yell "Digression!" at him. The interruptions especially intimidated a shy, nervous student named Richard Kinsella, who was giving a speech about his father's farm in Vermont. Richard *did* digress, telling about his uncle who had polio. Kinsella was interesting and excited in his story, but the boys cut him off with shouts of "Digression!" and Vinson gave him a D+ in the course. Holden prefers digressions. He often finds them more worthwhile than the original topic and digresses frequently, to the reader's benefit, in his own story.

Antolini disagrees that digressions are positive, arguing that "there's a time and place for everything." He then waxes philosophical, and at length, on Holden's character and the kinds of problems he may have in later life if he doesn't learn to conform. Inventing a strained and unfortunate metaphor, Antolini speaks of Holden's mind and education as if the boy were being fitted for a cheap suit. Holden is exhausted and yawns, unable to take any more. Perhaps it is Antolini who needs to learn that there is a time and a place for everything.

Most disturbing for Holden is the shock of waking to find Antolini patting him on the head. Holden's reaction, and his conclusion, may be excessive. Salinger allows the reader to decide, but it may be that Antolini is just drunk and awkwardly caring. After all, he is only patting Holden's head, not any other part of his body. For his part, Holden holds no doubt. He has seen more than his share of "perverty" behavior and is out of the apartment in short order.

Glossary

swanky ostentatiously stylish; expensive and showy.

lousy with dough here, oversupplied with money.

asthma a generally chronic disorder characterized by wheezing, coughing, difficulty in breathing, and a suffocating feeling, caused by an allergy to inhaled substances, stress, etc.

oiled up here, drunk, intoxicated.

sack bed.

digression a wandering from the main subject in talking or writing.

pedagogica of or characteristic of teachers or of teaching.

"It's a secret between he and I." Mr. Antolini surely knows that this example of poor grammar is one that Holden frequently slips into, using the subjective form of the pronouns instead of the objective. The correct form would be to say, "It's a secret between him and me."

Chapters 25 and 26

Summary

It is dawn on Monday as Holden leaves the Antolinis' apartment. He sleeps on a bench at the waiting room in Grand Central Station until about 9 a.m. Having second thoughts about Mr. Antolini's intentions, he wonders if he should have returned and stayed there. Walking up on Fifth Avenue, searching for an inexpensive restaurant in which to eat breakfast, he suddenly feels very anxious. Every time he steps down off the curb to cross a street, he thinks he may just keep falling and disappear. He asks his dead brother, Allie, to help him. Holden is physically and emotionally exhausted, sweating profusely despite the cold. He is near collapse.

In a final, awkward attempt to save himself, Holden decides to go "way out West" and live as a deaf-mute so he won't have to talk with people. Before leaving, he arranges to say good-bye to Phoebe. While he is with her, he decides to stop running and return home. In a brief final chapter, Holden concludes the story, telling us that he doesn't know what he thinks about everything that has happened, except that he misses the people he has told us about.

Commentary

Holden's anxiety as he crosses streets on Fifth Avenue is reminiscent of the feelings that he had on his way to Mr. Spencer's home near the end of Chapter 1. There, too, he felt that he was disappearing every time he crossed a road. The terror is related to the horror he feels toward mutability and death; it is not surprising that he calls on Allie for support. Allie has crossed over and knows the territory.

Holden's efforts concerning Phoebe seem ambiguous. He says he wants to see her before he leaves for the West. Because she is his most trusted living link to family, we have to wonder, even at this point, whether he really wants to say good-bye or whether he just longs for home. While delivering a note for Phoebe to the principal's office of her school, he sees that someone has written "Fuck you" on the wall by the stairs. This enrages him. Holden's own language is often salty, and Phoebe asked him to stop cursing when he visited her in the apartment, but he finds this word especially abhorrent and does not use it around his sister. It upsets him that innocent children must see such a thing. While waiting for Phoebe at the Museum of Art, he shows two boys an Egyptian tomb and sees the same obscenity on the wall even there. Holden concludes that there is no way to escape the ugliness of the world. Death is never far from his thoughts, and he guesses that someone probably will put the phrase on his tombstone, right under his name and the dates of his birth and death.

Character Insight

Holden's conversation with Phoebe results in his ultimate decision to go home. At first, she is determined to leave with him, having brought her essentials in one of his old suitcases. He says she cannot go. She refuses to return to school and insists that she does not even care about her role as Benedict Arnold or missing the play. Holden's decision to return home is suspiciously easy. Supposedly to get Phoebe to stop crying, he says he has changed his mind and is not leaving. He notices, though, that she is *not* crying at the time he makes this decision.

Literary Device

The touching final scene of Holden's long flashback, his story, takes place at the carousel in the park outside of the zoo. The great thing about a carousel, for Holden, is that it has beauty and music and even motion, but it doesn't go anywhere. Nothing really changes. However, not everyone wants things to stay the way they are. Symbolically, Phoebe and the other kids want to grab the gold ring hanging just beyond reach on each rotation. If they can grab the gold ring, they can win the prize, whatever that might be. In life, too, it is natural for young people to want to take a risk and try for something beyond what they have. Even Holden, taking an initial step toward maturity or change, concedes that, when kids long to "grab for the gold ring, you have to let them do it. . . . If they fall off, they fall off. . . ."

Theme

We get the feeling that Holden could stand there and watch Phoebe ride her "big, brown, beat-up-looking old horse" forever, even in the rain. The song the carousel plays is "Smoke Gets in Your Eyes," recalling the natural reaction of tears when smoke gets in people's eyes. Holden is so happy that he is "damned near bawling." Phoebe goes round and round, the music plays, and she looks "so damn *nice*" in her blue coat on that old wooden horse; for a moment, Holden's world is perfect.

Style & Language

That's all that Holden wants to tell us. He says that he did go home after being at the zoo with Phoebe. He got sick and ended up in California, but, for once, he doesn't want to go into the details. He doesn't know what the future holds, but he misses all the people in his past, even the jerks and bullies. "Don't ever tell anybody anything," he concludes. "If you do, you start missing everybody." Holden wishes that the story would never end. It would be perfect if it just kept going round and round, like that old carrousel.

Glossary

strong box a heavily made box or safe for storing valuables.

scraggy-looking lean; bony; skinny.

Salvation Army an international organization on semi-military lines, founded in England by William Booth in 1865 for religious and philanthropic purposes among the very poor.

Bloomingdale's a popular, Manhattan-based department store.

storm shoes all-weather boots.

Holland Tunnel a passageway connecting lower Manhattan with Jersey City, New Jersey, beneath the Hudson River.

double-decker bus a bus with an upper deck or floor.

carrousel a merry-go-round with various wooden or metal animals, especially ponies, serving as seats that go up and down.

affected behaving in an artificial way to impress people.

CHARACTER ANALYSES

The following character analyses delve into the physical, emotional, and psychological traits of the literary work's major characters so that you might better understand what motivates these characters. The writer of this study guide provides this scholarship as an educational tool by which you may compare your own interpretations of the characters. Before reading the character analyses that follow, consider first writing your own short essays on the characters as an exercise by which you can test your understanding of the original literary work. Then, compare your essays to those that follow, noting discrepancies between the two. If your essays appear lacking, that might indicate that you need to re-read the original literary work or re-familiarize yourself with the major characters.

Holden 78

Phoebe 80

Allie 81

D.B. 82

Mr. Antolini 83

Holden

Holden Caulfield, the 17-year-old narrator and protagonist of the novel, speaks to the reader directly from a mental hospital or sanitarium in southern California. The novel is a *frame story* (a story within a certain fictional framework) in the form of a long flashback. Holden wants to tell what happened over a two-day period the previous December, beginning on the Saturday afternoon of the traditional season-ending football game between his school, Pencey Prep, and Saxon Hall. Holden is 16 years old as the central story begins, tall at 6 feet 2½ inches, partially gray-haired, and woefully skinny. He has grown 6½ inches in just one year. He is out of shape because he smokes too much. His general health is poor. He is alternately depressed, confused, angry, anxious, perceptive, bigoted, resentful, thoughtful, kind, and horny. To put it simply, Holden is struggling.

To Holden, Pencey and the other prep schools that he has attended represent all that is artificial ("phony" is one of Holden's favorite words to describe this artificiality) and all that is despicable about any institution controlled by adults. The schools are filled with lies and cruelty, ranging in degree from the relatively harmless Pencey school motto ("Since 1888 we have been molding boys into splendid, clear-thinking young men.") to the brutally forced suicide of James Castle at Elkton Hills.

Holden resents the adult world and resists entry into it, but he has little choice. Society and his own body are telling him that it is time for him to change. He is attracted to the trappings of adulthood: booze, cigarettes, the *idea* of sex, and a kind of independence. But he despises the compromises, loss of innocence, absence of integrity, and loss of authenticity in the grown-up world. He seems best at the rites of passage (smoking and drinking) that are themselves artificial if not self-destructive. Despite his limited experience, his attitude toward women is actually admirable and mature. He stops making sexual advances when a girl says "No." He has trouble being very intimate unless he knows the girl well and likes her a lot. In his confusion, he sees this behavior as a weakness that may even call for psychotherapy. His interactions with the prostitute Sunny are comic as well as touching, partly because they are both adolescents trying to be adults. Although Sunny is the more frightening of the two, neither belongs there.

Holden is literally about to crash. Near the beginning as well as the end of the novel, he feels that he will disappear or fall into an abyss when he steps off a curb to cross a street. Sometimes when this happens, he calls on his dead brother, Allie, for help. Part of Holden's collapse is due to his inability to come to terms with death. Thoughts of Allie lying in his grave in the cemetery in the rain, surrounded by dead bodies and tombstones, haunt Holden. He wants time itself to stop. He wants beautiful moments to last forever, using as his model the displays in glass at the Museum of Natural History, in which the same people are shown doing the same things year after year. (Never mind that even museum displays change.) Holden's fears and desires are understandable, but his solution (avoiding reality) is impossible. Life *is* change. His feelings are typically adolescent, feelings shared by virtually everyone who is or ever has been his age. One of the reasons we like Holden is that he is so candid about how he feels.

Holden also struggles with family and class expectations. Like Salinger, his socioeconomic background is at least upper-middle class. His family and culture expect him to be reasonably successful at a prestigious prep school and move on to the Ivy League. Holden can't see himself in that role, so he seeks escape, but his plans are spontaneous fantasies that cannot work. First, he wants to run off with Sally Hayes and maybe get married. This frightens the practical, unimaginative Sally, who is more interested in social status than she is in Holden. Later, Holden decides to flee to the West where he will live as a deaf mute, ideal because he wouldn't have to talk with people. Holden is a romantic but a negative one. His imagined ventures are escapes from reality rather than ascensions toward a goal. The one exception is a beautiful but hopeless dream. When asked by Phoebe what he would like to be, Holden rejects standard choices such as a lawyer or a scientist. He says he would like to be "the catcher in the rye," standing by the edge of a cliff and keeping children, playing in an adjacent field of rye, from falling off.

Holden's alienation is disenchantment mingled with hope. He sees ugliness all around him, but he also sees beauty. The 6-year-old boy singing "If a body catch a body coming through the rye" as he marches down the street is, for Holden, a symbol of authenticity and possibility. He feels less depressed as he watches the boy. The sight of Phoebe on the carrousel is a kind of epiphany (a clarity of insight). It is one of those moments that he would like to keep forever. On the carrousel, there is movement, but the carrousel never actually goes anywhere: just round and round with Phoebe in her blue coat. It is beautiful, and, for a moment, even Holden feels joy.

This novel presents a coming-of-age story, but with a twist. The usual pattern in this genre of fiction is for the protagonist to begin in turmoil, struggle toward maturity, face various obstacles that initially defeat him but that he can overcome through *virtue* and *perseverance*, and eventually triumph. That is not Holden's story, however. Holden begins in turmoil, struggles in turmoil, has a moment of epiphany watching Phoebe at the carrousel, and eventually suffers physical and emotional collapse.

Holden does evolve toward the end of the novel. His acceptance of Phoebe's need to "grab for the gold ring" indicates that he sees her as a maturing individual who must be allowed to live her own life and take her own risks. At this point, he finally sees that children have to do this, and adults must let them. That's a step forward from believing that he must be their protector. For better or worse, Holden's own maturation has begun. He seems ready to surrender to the inevitability of growing up. He is exhausted, physically and emotionally, ready to go home and collapse.

Holden may or may not have progressed enough, learned enough, matured enough at the sanitarium to make it in the future. We can cheer for him, but we can't know what will happen. Salinger does not spoon-feed the reader a "happy" ending, which is all the better for readers of the novel. As Holden says in the final chapter, "I mean how do you know what you're going to do till you *do* it?"

Phoebe

Holden's 10-year-old sister, Phoebe, is bright, pretty, mature beyond her years, sane, and his most trusted link to family. She has red hair and is "roller-skate skinny," a metaphor that, Salinger seems to be saying, is like jazz; you either understand it when you hear it, or you never will. Phoebe's favorite movie is the Hitchcock film *The 39 Steps* (1935); she has committed the dialogue to memory. She is successful in school, her best course being spelling. She is the one who corrects Holden concerning the words to the Robert Burns poem that is the source of the novel's title. In her spare time, she writes fiction featuring a girl detective, an orphan named Hazle Weatherfield. Phoebe later adopts "Weatherfield" as her own middle name. She likes elephants and has red ones on her blue pajamas. She studies belching with a friend named Phyllis; her best friend, Alice, is teaching Phoebe to induce a fever artificially by crossing her legs, holding her breath, and thinking of something very hot. She conscientiously promises not to burn Holden while demonstrating her trick.

Holden's adolescence and his confusion complicate the relationship with Phoebe. While she sometimes seems to be his best friend, at other times he is acutely aware of her sexuality or need for independence. Twice (Chapters 10 and 21) he says that she can sometimes be *too* affectionate. Although he is capable of giving her "a pinch on the behind," which is "sticking way out in the breeze," he knows better than to put his hand on her shoulder at the wrong time. When Phoebe rides the carrousel, Holden realizes that there are times when kids want to try to grab the gold ring, symbolically taking a chance in life, and he must allow her the freedom to do that, even though she may fall. That realization is a big step for Holden. All things considered, the relationship between Holden and Phoebe seems healthy and normal for caring siblings. It is in flux, as is everything in life, and Holden may regret that. But he shows he has grown when he realizes that Phoebe can't stay 10 years old forever.

For her part, Phoebe sometimes sees right through her brother. She realizes early in his visit that he has been expelled from Pencey. On the other hand, some of Holden's darker thoughts are beyond her. She can't fathom why he is so self-destructive or why he doesn't just succeed in school the way she does. When he bares his soul to tell her of his dream of being "the catcher in the rye," she is quiet for a long time but then simply states, in reference to his expulsion, "Daddy's going to kill you," illustrating that despite their great friendship and connection, Phoebe is still only 10 years old and cannot be expected to understand the true meaning of Holden's words.

Allie

Although he has been dead for about three years, Allie is a mystic presence in the novel. Holden thinks of him often and speaks to him when things are darkest in his life. Allie is associated with the theme of death, but his role is not that simple. He also represents hope and the gifted innocence of childhood, which is tenuous and sometimes short-lived. Holden clearly loves his brother. Only two years apart in age, they were close friends.

Allie died of leukemia at the Caulfields' summer home in Maine on July 18, 1946. He was 11 years old; Holden was 13. Holden, distraught over the loss of his brother, broke his hand punching the windows out of the garage of their summer home. Holden missed Allie's funeral because he was in the hospital, apparently for psychiatric evaluation as well as for attention to his hand. Depending on the date of Holden's birthday and his precision with numbers, that was about four years before Holden tells the story (at age 17) from the sanitarium in California and perhaps three and a half years before Holden (age 16) leaves Pencey. Allie was the most intelligent as well as the "nicest" member of the family. His connection to Holden was intense. The older brother could sense when Allie was in the vicinity, although he credits Allie's red hair for that. Holden would get a hunch that Allie was there; when he turned around, there Allie was.

Allie's left-handed baseball glove is a symbol of his unique personality as well as Holden's love for his brother. The unique part of the glove is that Allie wrote poems all over it, in green ink. He did that so he would have something to read when he was in the baseball field and the game was boring. Holden keeps the glove with him and has it at Pencey. It is, of course, misguided to think that the boorish Stradlater, Holden's roommate, could understand or appreciate the essay that Holden writes about the glove. Stradlater wants something descriptive to hand in to his English teacher and is too lazy and dull to do the work himself. He asks Holden to write it. Telling someone like Stradlater about the glove is a sacrilege. Allie is more than a brother to Holden. In Holden's chaotic cosmos, he is an angelic presence, a connection to death but also to hope.

D.B.

Holden's older brother is one representative of the aesthetic theme of the genuine artist who sells out. Holden feels that D.B. was a truly "terrific" short-story writer before going to Hollywood to write scripts, drive Jaguars, date gorgeous women, and make money. "The Secret Goldfish," a story about a kid who buys a goldfish with his own money and won't let anyone else look at it, is Holden's favorite short story written by his brother.

Holden dislikes the movies because he thinks that they are "phony" and manipulative; he feels that his brother has prostituted himself by becoming a screenwriter. Like Salinger, D.B. served extensively in World War II, landed in France on D-Day, and was in Europe for the duration. He was disillusioned by the war and especially the military. Perhaps that cynicism was part of his decision to become a screenwriter.

Mr. Antolini

One of the more controversial characters in the novel, Mr. Antolini was Holden's favorite teacher at Elkton Hills. Holden admires and respects him because Antolini is not only intellectual and perceptive, but he has a heart. When James Castle committed suicide, it was Antolini who carried his bloody, broken body all the way to the infirmary. Now an English instructor at New York University, Antolini initially is a role model, a big brother (approximately the same age as D.B.), to Holden.

It is all the more confusing, then, for Holden to see that the drunken Antolini can be as boring a windbag as Spencer, and frightening as well. Holden may overreact to the situation, perhaps even misjudge it, when he awakens to find Antolini patting him on the head on the night he stays in the Antolinis' apartment, but it clearly is at least an uncomfortable and inappropriate situation. Holden is disillusioned. His short night at the Antolinis' has taught him another of life's painful lessons: His golden idol has feet of clay.

CRITICAL ESSAYS

On the pages that follow, the writer of this study guide provides critical scholarship on various aspects of Salinger's *The Catcher in the Rye*. These interpretive essays are intended solely to enhance your understanding of the original literary work; they are supplemental materials and are not to replace your reading of *The Catcher in the Rye*. When you're finished reading *The Catcher in the Rye*, and prior to your reading this study guide's critical essays, consider making a bulleted list of what you think are the most important themes and symbols. Write a short paragraph under each bullet explaining why you think that theme or symbol is important; include at least one short quote from the original literary work that supports your contention. Then, test your list and reasons against those found in the following essays. Do you include themes and symbols that the study guide author doesn't? If so, this self test might indicate that you are well on your way to understanding original literary work. But if not, perhaps you will need to re-read *The Catcher in the Rye*.

The Major Themes of *The Catcher in the Rye* 86

Major Symbols of *The Catcher in the Rye* 89

The Coming-of-Age Genre 91

The Major Themes of *The Catcher in the Rye*

Themes in literary works are recurring, unifying subjects or ideas, motifs that allow us to understand more deeply the characters and their world. In *The Catcher in the Rye*, the major themes reflect the values and motivations of the characters. Some of these themes are outlined in the following sections.

Innocence

As its title indicates, the dominating theme of *The Catcher in the Rye* is the protection of innocence, especially of children. For most of the book, Holden sees this as a primary virtue. It is very closely related to his struggle against growing up. Holden's enemy is the adult world and the cruelty and artificiality that it entails. The people he admires all represent or protect innocence. He thinks of Jane Gallagher, for example, not as a maturing young woman but as the girl with whom he used to play checkers. He goes out of his way to tell us that he and Jane had no sexual relationship. Quite sweetly, they usually just held hands. Holden comforted Jane when she was distressed, and it bothers him that Jane may have been subjected to sexual advances from her drunken stepfather or from her date, Holden's roommate, Stradlater.

Holden's secret goal is to be "the catcher in the rye." In this metaphor, he envisions a field of rye standing by a dangerous cliff. Children play in the field with joy and abandon. If they should come too close to the edge of the cliff, however, Holden is there to catch them. His attitude seems to shift near the end of the novel when he realizes that Phoebe and other children must be allowed to "grab for the gold ring," to choose their own risks and take them, even though their attempts may be dangerous.

Death

Death is another consistent theme in the novel. It is continually implied by the presence of Holden's younger brother's spirit, even though Allie has been dead for about three years. When Holden fears for his own existence, such as when he feels that he might disappear, he speaks to Allie. He is haunted by the thought of Allie in the rainy cemetery surrounded by tombstones and dead people. Holden associates death with the mutability of time. He wishes that everything could just stay the way it is, that time could stand still, especially when something beautiful happens. When he compares this to the displays under glass at the museum, Holden seems to be rejecting life itself. Life *is* change. Aging and mutability are inevitable. It isn't just that society wants Holden to grow up; his own biological condition insists that he become an adult. When he resists change, Holden is fighting the biological clock that eventually will result in old age and death. He also resists simply growing up. Although we may admire his candor and even sometimes identify with his adolescent wish, we are left to conclude that Holden's way leads to considerable frustration and, eventually, madness.

The Authentic versus the Artificial

Holden's aesthetics are entertaining, but they also tell us a good deal about his worldview. He sees much of life as a conflict between the authentic and the artificial, which is directly related to his attitude toward children and his resistance to the adult world. When Holden sees the 6-year-old child marching down the street singing, "If a body catch a body coming through the rye," he is uplifted because of the authenticity of the scene. The boy is not trying to please anyone; he is merely expressing his passion of the moment. D.B.'s short stories fall into the same category. They are quiet, private, an author's expression of his own truth without concern for reward. Estelle Fletcher, the black artist who sings "Little Shirley Beans" on the recording that Holden buys for Phoebe, is another adult who gets it right. Holden likes her jazz style, saying she "sings it very Dixieland and whorehouse, and it doesn't sound at all mushy." He appreciates the fact that she avoids sentimentality and doesn't cater to the audience by making the song "sound cute as hell."

On the other hand, when Ernie plays his piano at his nightclub in Greenwich Village, or when D.B. writes screenplays for Hollywood, or when various actors compromise their talents to please an audience, Holden can't stand it. These adult manipulations are, for him, the same as prostitution. The artists have sold out—for money or fame or just for applause. Nor can he tolerate what he sees as emotional manipulations in literature. Romance magazines with "lean-jawed guys named David" and "a lot of phony girls named Linda or Marcia" usually set Holden to "puking," although he does sometimes read them on the train. Hemingway's *A Farewell to Arms*, which has a great reputation as an antiwar novel, also strikes him as manipulative and artificial. So do most films, especially sentimental war films. In the end, he seems to distrust the corrupting potential of the relationship between artist and audience, especially among adults.

Sexual Confusion

Sexual confusion is another of the consistent themes in *The Catcher in the Rye*. It is not unusual for any of us to be concerned about sex as adolescents, but Holden is especially so. He has the usual biological yearnings but has mixed feelings about how he should respond to them. Although he is a romantic, he still admits that he is sexually driven. It is to Holden's credit that he respects what girls say when they ask him to stop making advances, even though he has heard the usual rumors that they don't always mean it. When a girl says she wants to stop, Holden stops. "No" means "No" for Holden Caulfield. Unfortunately, Holden seems to think this is one of his weaknesses. During the encounter with Sunny, the prostitute, Holden decides that he simply does not want to go through with the act of sex. While talking later with Carl Luce at the Wicker Bar, Holden wonders if he needs psychoanalysis because he has difficulty being intimate with a girl unless he really cares about her. Luce, who likes to pose as a sophisticate, lacks the maturity or good sense to tell Holden that these feelings are admirable.

On the other hand, Holden is unusually concerned about homosexual males (whom he calls "flits"). He thinks that all homoerotic behavior is "perverty," lumping it together with bestiality (or at least accepting the fact that Carl Luce has this view).

Although Holden is understandably bothered by Mr. Antolini's odd behavior at the apartment, he might be over-reacting. Salinger is unclear about the former teacher's motive. Holden and the readers might notice that the teacher pats him on the head, not the genitals.

Thinking about major themes can be helpful to the reader. However, as readers of any work of fiction (especially with a novel as complex and richly ambiguous as *The Catcher in the Rye*) we need to be careful not to try to define or dissect too much. Most interpretations of the novel are debatable. *The Catcher in the Rye* remains a force in literature precisely because it may mean many things to many different people.

Major Symbols of *The Catcher in the Rye*

A literary symbol is something, often an object, that stands for a significant concept or series of ideas. Sometimes it is emblematic of the values of the characters. Some of the most important symbols in *The Catcher in the Rye* are outlined in the following sections.

Preparatory School Life

Pencey Prep and Elkton Hills are examples of institutions that serve as symbols. For Holden, the schools represent the phony, cruel world of those who run them. Even the advertisements for Pencey Prep are misleading. They feature "some hot shot guy on a horse" performing equestrian feats. Holden says he has never even *seen* a horse at Pencey. The school's motto is equally repulsive to Holden: "Since 1888 we have been molding boys into splendid, clear-thinking young men." Holden can think of perhaps two boys who fit that description, and they probably came to Pencey that way. For Holden, a more typical example of the Pencey preppie is his roommate, Ward Stradlater, a boorish womanizer who gets by on superficial good looks and fake charm. Holden is being expelled for poor academic performance, but Stradlater wants to cheat by having Holden do his English theme for him since Holden does write well.

Even more serious is the cruelty that Holden has seen at prep schools. As he tells Phoebe, "You never saw so many mean guys in your life." Holden dislikes the exclusivity and the prejudice against those who are neither attractive nor hip. He is ashamed of himself for going along with the crowd and joining a secret fraternity. Although James Castle's brutally forced suicide took place at Elkton Hills, we get the idea that it could have happened at Pencey Prep just as easily. For Holden, the two schools are emblematic of a corrupt system designed by privileged adults and catering to boys who want to join their ranks. Part of Holden's dilemma is that he struggles so hard against a system into which he was born.

Allie's Baseball Glove

Allie's left-handed baseball glove is a physically smaller but significant symbol in the novel. It represents Holden's love for his deceased brother as well as Allie's authentic uniqueness. Allie covered the glove with poems written in green ink so that he would have something to read when things got boring in the baseball field. This mitt is not a catcher's mitt; it is a fielder's glove. Holden has shown it to only one person outside the family: Jane Gallagher. When he writes a descriptive theme about the glove for Stradlater to turn in for his English assignment, of course the insensitive roommate does not understand.

Holden's Red Hunting Cap

Holden's red hunting cap is another small artifact of symbolic meaning. He bought it for one dollar in New York on the Saturday morning when he lost the fencing equipment. The cap is practical at times but is foolish-looking, with its extra-long bill and earflaps. It represents Holden's delightful attraction to unusual qualities, in objects as well as people, that others might miss. He realizes that the hat is unfashionable and occasionally is careful about who sees it, but he loves it anyway. He likes to wear it with the bill pointing to the back, as a baseball *catcher* might. For Holden, it is a reading cap as much as a protection against the cold. Because this is a hunting cap, we might speculate on what it is that Holden is hunting.

Radio City Music Hall

Radio City Music Hall, with its Christmas show, the Rockettes, and the painfully sentimental war movie, symbolizes much of what Holden despises about inauthentic art that panders to the audience. Holden sees nothing religious or beautiful about the stage show. He thinks that "old Jesus probably would've puked if He could see it." The legendary precision of the Rockettes' chorus line leaves Holden cold. The movie is worse, because it manipulates the audience into a sentimental glorification of war and the military, which Holden despises. He couldn't even stand the Boy Scouts.

The Carrousel's Gold Ring

A carrousel is a sort of motorized merry-go-round with seats that look like various animals, such as painted ponies, move up and down. Designed for children, some carrousels have a gold ring, perhaps 4 or 5 inches in diameter, hanging on the outer edge where the children might, with some difficulty, reach out and grab it as they pass by. The child who grabs the ring wins a prize of some sort: perhaps a free ride or a stuffed animal. However, there is some risk in going for the gold ring. The rider might even fall. So the gold ring represents a hope, a dream, and the chances that we must take to grab it. It is a major step for Holden to accept that kids will grab for the gold ring and adults must let them. It is part of life and part of growing up.

The Coming-of-Age Genre

Genre is a French word (pronounced ZHON-ruh) meaning a particular kind or type of art or literature. One popular genre of American fiction is the coming-of-age story. A typical example might be Robert Lipsyte's novel *The Contender*, in which a young protagonist, near Holden's age, begins in turmoil, struggles toward maturity, meets various obstacles that initially defeat him but that he finds he can overcome through virtue and perseverance, and eventually triumphs. Lipsyte's novel is more interesting than most because the author uses a sport, boxing, to help the protagonist mature, but the main character does not triumph in the *sport*. He triumphs in *life*. This, however, is not Holden's story.

The Catcher in the Rye is a coming-of-age novel with a twist. Holden does not follow the usual pattern. He begins in turmoil, struggles in turmoil, has a moment of epiphany (clarity of insight) watching Phoebe at the carrousel, but eventually suffers physical and emotional collapse. Holden *does* change toward the end of the book. His acceptance of Phoebe's need to "grab for the gold ring" indicates that he sees her as a maturing individual who must be allowed to live her own life and take her own chances, even though she may fail or fall. Children must do this, and adults must let them. For better or worse, Holden is beginning to grow up; but he is far from any kind of triumph. He will go home and soon collapse, resulting in his stay at the sanitarium in California. We cannot know how he will be in the future. Salinger does not spoon-feed the reader a "happy" ending. In that way, the novel is more realistic, more lifelike and authentic than some representatives of the genre.

CliffsNotes Review

Use this CliffsNotes Review to test your understanding of the original text, and reinforce what you've learned in this book. After you work through the review and essay questions, identify the quote section, and the fun and useful practice projects, you're well on your way to understanding a comprehensive and meaningful interpretation of *The Catcher in the Rye*.

Q&A

1. Allie died of _____ on the date of _____ .

2. Ward Stradlater's date on Saturday night is with _____.

3. On the train to New York, Holden meets _____, the mother of _____.

4. Holden is concerned because his brother D.B. has pursued a profession as _____.

5. On their Sunday date, Holden and Sally Hayes attend a matinee and then go to _____.

6. Mr. Antolini awakens and alarms Holden by _____.

7. Jane Gallagher's unusual approach to checkers is to _____ _____.

8. In the Christmas pageant at school, Phoebe is to play the part of _____.

9. Holden discusses Shakespeare's *Romeo and Juliet* with _____ _____.

10. Holden's favorite short story by his older brother, D.B., is _____ _____.

Answers: (1) leukemia; July 18, 1946. (2) Jane Gallagher. (3) Mrs. Morton; his classmate Ernest. (4) a screenwriter in Hollywood. (5) Radio City to skate. (6) patting Holden on the head. (7) keep her kings in the back row. (8) Benedict Arnold. (9) two nuns who are teachers. (10) "The Secret Goldfish."

Identify the Quote: Find Each Quote in The Catcher in The Rye

1. It was just that she looked so damn *nice*, the way she kept going around and around, in her blue coat and all. God, I wish you could've been there.

2. If you really want to hear about it, the first thing you'll probably want to know is where I was born, and what my lousy childhood was like, and how my parents were occupied and all before they had me, and all that David Copperfield kind of crap, but I don't feel like going into it, if you want to know the truth.

3. What I have to do, I have to catch everybody if they start to go over the cliff—I mean if they're running and they don't look where they're going I have to come out from somewhere and *catch* them. That's all I'd do all day.

4. The funny thing is, though, I was sort of thinking of something else while I shot the bull. I live in New York, and I was thinking about the lagoon in Central Park, down near Central Park South. I was wondering if it would be frozen over when I got home, and if it was, where did the ducks go.

5. The thing that was descriptive about it, though, was that he had poems written all over the fingers and the pocket and everywhere. In green ink.

Answers: (1) Holden describes Phoebe on the carrousel at the end of Chapter 25. It is a rare moment of happiness for Holden before he must go on to face the adult world; he sometimes wishes such moments could last forever. (2) The opening sentence of the novel, spoken by Holden, establishes him as a narrator outside of the traditional mode. (3) Holden is telling Phoebe what he would really like to *be*—the catcher in the rye—during their visit in his parents' apartment in Chapter 22, demonstrating his concern for the protection of innocence. (4) While speaking with Mr. Spencer in Chapter 2, Holden's mind drifts. Typically, he digresses, but he indicates his compassion by worrying about the ducks and where they go in the winter. (5) In Chapter 5, Holden describes his deceased brother Allie's baseball glove, which symbolizes Holden's love for his brother as well as Allie's unique spirit.

Essay Questions

1. Discuss the novel as a coming-of-age story. How does Holden's character change during the course of the novel?

2. Consider one of the following as symbols: the gold ring, Pencey Prep, or Holden's hunting cap.

3. Discuss the theme of death in the novel, citing specific events or passages.

4. Read one other coming-of-age novel, such as Mark Twain's *The Adventures of Huckleberry Finn* or Robert Lipsyte's *The Contender*, and compare the protagonists, settings, symbols, and themes with those in *The Catcher in the Rye*.

5. Based on what you know of Holden, what do you think his future will be?

6. Discuss Holden's relationship with Phoebe citing specifics from their conversations.

7. Why does Holden want to be the catcher in the rye? What are the positive and negative aspects of his fantasy?

Practice Projects

1. You are an investigative reporter for the *New York Times*, assigned to look into charges of impropriety at prestigious area prep schools. Choose three characters from the novel and write an interview with them, including your questions as well as their responses. Have friends read the parts of the prep school characters and record your interview on video or audio tape.

2. Choose a scene from the novel and dramatize it for the rest of your class. The production will require putting the scene in play form (freely adapting according to inspiration), assigning roles, directing, and staging the production. Follow the performance with a discussion of the novel's themes.

3. Create a Web site to introduce *The Catcher in the Rye* to other readers. Design pages to intrigue and inform your audience, and invite other readers to post their thoughts and responses to their reading of the novel.

CliffsNotes Resource Center

The learning doesn't need to stop here. CliffsNotes Resource Center shows you the best of the best—links to the best information in print and online about the author and/or related works. And don't think that this is all we've prepared for you; we've put all kinds of pertinent information at www.cliffsnotes.com. Look for all the terrific resources at your favorite bookstore or local library and on the Internet. When you're online, make your first stop www.cliffsnotes.com where you'll find more incredibly useful information about *The Catcher in the Rye*.

Books

This CliffsNotes book provides a meaningful interpretation of *The Catcher in the Rye* published by Wiley Publishing, Inc. If you are looking for information about the author and/or related works, check out these other publications:

At Home in the World: A Memoir, by Joyce Maynard, is an account of the author's 1972 affair, at the age of eighteen, with Salinger. Along with numerous bizarre details, she reports that the author had two completed, unpublished novels kept in a vault. New York: Picador USA, 1998.

The Catcher in the Rye: Innocence Under Pressure, by Sanford Pinsker, is an excellent resource for students of *The Catcher in the Rye*. It is a thorough and reasonable critique, with a chronology and a briefly annotated bibliography. Part of the Twayne's Masterwork Studies series. New York: Simon & Schuster, 1993.

In Search of J.D. Salinger, by Ian Hamilton, is the story of a difficult attempt to write an unauthorized biography of Salinger as well as a comment on the fiction writer's life. Court proceedings regarding the book set remarkable precedents. New York: Random House, 1988.

J.D. Salinger, edited by Harold Bloom, the distinguished critic and professor at Yale University, presents, chronologically, Bloom's selection of the "best criticism" on Salinger from 1958 through 1984, with a chronology and an introduction by the editor. New York: Chelsea House, 1987.

J.D. Salinger, by James E. Miller, Jr., is one of the best of the early appreciations of Salinger. It places him at the top of the list of American fiction writers dealing with post-World War II themes of alienation. Part of the University of Minnesota Pamphlets on American Writers series. Minneapolis: University of Minnesota Press, 1965.

J.D. Salinger, Revisited, by Warren French, is a very helpful continuation of the analysis of an early Salinger scholar. The book includes a detailed chronology and annotated bibliography. Part of the Twayne's United States Authors series. Boston: Twayne Publishers, 1988.

New Essays on The Catcher in the Rye, edited by Jack Salzman, provides five helpful essays, including Peter Shaw's insights on the themes of love and death in the novel. The editor's introduction presents a thorough consideration of the novel's initial critical reception. New York: Cambridge University Press, 1991.

Studies in J.D. Salinger: Reviews, Essays, and Critiques of The Catcher in the Rye and Other Fiction, edited by Marvin Laser and Norman Fruman, is an excellent collection of assorted approaches to the novel. The volume includes a helpful introduction by the editors. New York: Odyssey Press, 1963

It's easy to find books published by Wiley Publishing, Inc. You'll find them in your favorite bookstores (on the Internet and at a store near you). We also have three Web sites that you can use to read about all the books we publish:

- www.cliffsnotes.com
- www.dummies.com
- www.wiley.com

Internet

Check out these Web resources for more information about J.D. Salinger and *The Catcher in the Rye*:

New York Times **Book Archives** http://www.nytimes.com After registering with this free Web site, you can access the book section find numerous reviews, news articles, and interviews, about J.D. Salinger and his work. This is an excellent, stable resource.

Page Index for *The Catcher in the Rye,* www.dimensional.com/ ~suzannem/catcher/ — A helpful if incomplete index, this lists various words or names and the pages on which they can be found in the Little, Brown paperback edition of the novel.

Salinger.org, www.salinger.org — A collaborative, online Salinger Web site, offering bibliography, information on characters, opinion, anecdotes, and news regarding the author and his works.

Western Canon University J.D. Salinger *Catcher in the Rye* **Quad,** moby-dicks.com/salinger/common.html — Chat rooms and lecture halls are offered on a variety of subjects concerning Salinger, the novel, characters in the novel, and other Salinger works.

Next time you're on the Internet, don't forget to drop by www.cliffs notes.com. We created an online Resource Center that you can use today, tomorrow, and beyond.

Films and Other Recordings

MAYNARD, JOYCE. *At Home in the World: A Memoir* (abridged). Read by the author. Audiocassette. Soudelux Audio Publishing, 1998. An account of the author's 1972 affair, at the age of eighteen, with Salinger. Along with numerous bizarre details, she reports that the author had two completed, unpublished novels kept in a vault.

The 39 Steps. Dir. Alfred Hitchcock. Perf. Robert Donat and Madeleine Carroll. Gaumont-British Picture Corporation, Ltd., 1935. The film memorized by Holden Caulfield's younger sister, Phoebe.

Magazines and Journals

EPPES, BETTY. "What I Did Last Summer." *Paris Review*, 80 (24 July 1981): 221–39. This article is of interest as a biographical insight. Eppes managed to get an interview with Salinger in Windsor, Vermont, in June 1980, involving unauthorized photographs and audiotape.

FOSBURGH, LACEY. "J.D. Salinger Speaks about His Silence." *New York Times*, 3 November 1974: 1, 69. Protesting the unauthorized publication of a collection of his short stories, Salinger initiated a telephone interview with a *New York Times* representative.

"J.D. Salinger Special Number." *Modern Fiction Studies*, 12, no. 3 (Autumn 1966). Seven worthwhile articles, including "Zen and Salinger" by Bernice and Sanford Goldstein, plus a bibliography.

Index

NUMBERS

39 Steps, The, 98

A

Ackley, Robert, 18, 29
Adventures of Huckleberry Finn, The, 13, 22
Antolini, 17
    character analysis, 83
    character insight, 70, 71
    lecturing Holden on his character, 71
    patting Holden's head, 71
Antolini, Lillian, 17
appeal of novel, 14
At Home in the World: A Memoir, 5, 96, 98
authentic versus artificial, theme of, 23, 54,
    64, 87, 88

B

banned books, 10
baseball glove, Allie's, 33, 82, 89
beats, 11
Bernice, 18, 42
biographical interpretations of novel, 23
blacklists, 10
Bloom, Harold, 96
Breit, Harvey, 13
Burnett, Whit, 2
Burroughs, William S., 11

C

carrousel, 74
Castle, James, 18, 65
catcher in the rye, Holden's desire to be, 66
*Catcher in the Rye: Innocence Under Pressure,
The,* 12, 38, 96
Catcher in the Rye, The, 13
    appeal of, 14
    banning of, 10
    biographical interpretations of novel, 23
    characters, list of, 16–18
    condemnation of, 13
    cultural issues during, 11

economy during, 8
financial concerns of family, lack of, 9
historical setting, 8
narrative style, 22
New York City and, 12
polio and, 11, 12
political issues during, 9
publication of, 4
repression, spirit of, 10
reviews of, 12, 13, 14
synopsis of, 14, 16
The Adventures of Huckleberry Finn
    compared to, 22
Caulfield, Allie, 17, 49
    baseball glove, 33, 82, 89
    character analysis, 81
Caulfield, D.B., 17
    character analysis, 82
    sell out, as, 45
Caulfield, Holden, 16
    adults, resentment and imitation of, 41
    aesthetics of, 51, 53, 54, 59
    Allie, talking out loud to, 49
    Allie's death, obsession with, 62
    Antolini patting head, reaction to, 71
    anxiousness of, 73
    balance between function and collapse,
        maintaining, 68
    betrayal, resentment of, 51
    carelessness of, 23
    carrousel and, 74
    catcher in the rye, desire to be, 66
    character analysis, 78, 79
    character flaws, revealing, 25, 26
    character insight, 33, 38, 43, 47, 49, 52,
        59, 60, 66, 70
    compassion of, 26
    cowardice, 47
    decision not to leave home, 74
    drunken phone call to Sally, 61
    ducks, search for, 61
    efforts to see Phoebe, 73, 74
    epiphany, moment of, 80
    exaggerations of, 29
    expulsion of, 23
    Faith Cavendish, attempt at intimacy
        with, 39
    fighting ability, inept, 47
    Freudian slip, 38
    friendship, importance of, 49
    hunting cap, 29, 90
    innocence, protection of, 66
    irresponsibility of, 23

Caulfield, Holden *(continued)*
  Jane, feelings for, 43
  lies about Ernie, 38
  life partners, thoughts on, 56
  losing himself, feelings of, 24
  loyalty, importance of, 49
  Luce, relationship with, 59
  lying, habit of, 29
  madman, identification with, 49
  Maurice, fight with, 50
  memory of James Castle, 65
  motivation in talking to Mrs. Morrow, 38
  movies, opinion of, 54
  as narrator, 22
  nuns, donation to, 52
  people, concern for, 23
  Phoebe as soulmate of, 41
  Phoebe, stability through, 64
  Salinger, example of difference from, 29
  Sally Hayes, relationship with, 51, 57
  sex and, 47, 48
  sexuality of, 39, 60
  socioeconomic background, 9
  Sunny and, 47
  theater, opinion of, 54, 57
Caulfield, Phoebe, 16
  character analysis, 80–82
  character insight, 41, 63, 68, 69
  Holden as soulmate of, 41
Cavendish, Faith, 18, 39
character analysis
  Allie Caulfield, 81
  Antolini, 83
  D.B. Caulfield, 82
  Holden Caulfield, 78, 79
  Phoebe Caulfield, 80–82
character insight
  Antolini, 70, 71
  Holden Caulfield, 33, 38, 43, 47, 49, 52,
    59, 60, 66, 70
  Horwitz, 45
  Jane Gallagher, 43, 44
  Phoebe Caulfield, 41, 63, 68, 69
  Sally Hayes, 57
  Ward Stradlater, 31, 35
characters, list of, 16–18
Charlene, 17
child singing in street, 54
Collier's, 3
coming-of-age genre, 91
Complete Uncollected Short Stories of J.D.
  Salinger, The, 5
condemnation of novel, 13

Contender, The, 91
Cosmopolitan, 3
cultural issues, 11

D

death, theme of, 28, 86, 87
Douglas, Claire, 3

E

economic issues, 8
Eisenhower, Dwight, 9
epiphany, 80
Ernie, 18, 38, 45
Esquire, 3
essay questions, 94

F

Fadiman, Clifton, 13
first rejection rights, 3
flashback, story as, 78
frame story , 78
"Franny", 4
Franny and Zooey, 5
French, Warren, 4, 97
Freudian slips, 38, 48
Fruman, Norman, 97

G

Gallagher, Jane, 17, 43, 44
GI Bill of Rights, 8
Ginsberg, Allen, 11
Glass, Seymour, 3
Glory and the Dream: A Narrative History of
  America, The, 9
gold ring of carrousel, symbolism of, 90

H

Hamilton, Ian, 4, 96
Hamlet, 54
"Hapworth 16, 1924", 5
Hayes, Sally, 17
  character insight, 57
  Holden, relationship with, 51, 57
historical setting, 8
Horwitz, 18, 45
Howl, 11
humor, death and, 28

hunting cap, Holden's red
    symbolism of, 29, 90

I

In Search of J.D. Salinger, 96
innocence, theme of, 66, 86
irony
    gray hair, Holden having, 25
    height of Holden, 25
    Jim Steele, 48
    Sunny, 48

J

J.D. Salinger, 96, 97
J.D. Salinger, Revisited, 97

K

Kerouac, Jack, 11
Kinsella, Richard, 71

L

Laverne, 18, 42
Levitt, William J., 11
Levittowns, 11
Lipsyte, Robert, 91
literary symbol. *See* symbols
Luce, Carl, 59

M

magazine articles, 98
Manchester, William, 9
Margolic, David, 4
Marty, 18, 42
Maurice, 18, 50
Maynard, Joyce, 5, 96
McCarthy, Joseph, 9
Mercutio, 51
Miller, James E., 97
Morrow, Mrs., 18, 38
Mother, 17
Museum of Natural History, 54
My Foolish Heart, 5

N

Naked Lunch, 11
narrative style of book, 22
New Essays on The Catcher in the Rye, 97
New York City, 12
New York Times, 3
New York Times Book Archives, 97
New Yorker magazine, 3, 4
Nine Stories, 5
novella, 3
nuclear threat, 10
nuns, 51, 52

O

On the Road, 11
online resources, 97
Oral Expression class, 71
Ossenburger, 18

P

Page Index for *The Catcher in the Rye,* 97
Pencey Prep, 23
    fraudulence of, example of, 33
    symbolism of, 89
    Valley Forge Military Academy compared
        to, 23
"Perfect Day for Bananafish, A," 3
Pinsker, Sanford, 12, 38, 96
polio, 11, 12
political issues, 9
practice projects, 95
preparatory school life, symbolism of, 89
prostitutes, 48

Q

quotes, 94

R

Radio City Music Hall, symbolism of, 59, 90
"Raise High the Roof Beam, Carpenters,"
    4, 5
repression, 10
review questions and answers, 93
reviews of novel, 12–14

S

Salinger, Doris, 2
Salinger, J.D.
    birth of, 2
    books written by, 5
    career highlights, 4
    Columbia University, 2
    divorce of, 3
    early career, 3
    education, 2
    interview with, 3
    as literary recluse, 4
    marriage, first, 3
    marriage, second, 3
    New York University, 2
    personal background, 2
    short stories written by, 4, 5
    unauthorized biography of, 4
    Ursinus College, 2
Salinger, Margaret Ann, 3
Salinger, Marie, 2
Salinger, Matthew, 3
Salinger, Sol, 2
Salinger.org, 98
Salzman, Jack, 97
Saturday Evening Post, 3
sexual confusion, theme of, 88
"Seymour: An Introduction," 4, 5
Simmons, Lillian, 18, 46
Spencer, Mr., 17, 26
Spencer, Mrs., 17, 25
Stern, James, 13
Story magazine, 2
Stradlater, Ward, 17
    character insight, 31, 35
    sloppiness of, 31
    superficiality of, 35
    womanizer, as, 35
Studies in J.D. Salinger: Reviews, Essays and Critques of The Catcher in the Rye and Other Fiction, 97
Sunny, 18, 47, 48, 50
Sylvia, 3
symbols
    baseball glove, Allie's, 33, 82, 89
    gold ring of carrousel, 90
    hunting cap, Holden's red, 29, 90
    preparatory school life, 89
    Radio City Music Hall, 90
synopsis, 14, 16

T

theater, 57
themes
    authentic versus artificial, 23, 54, 64, 87, 88
    compatibility, 56
    death, 28, 46, 53, 54, 86, 87
    innocence, 33, 36, 86
    sexual confusion, 88
Truman, Harry S., 9

U

"Uncle Wiggily in Connecticut," 5

V

Valley Forge Military Academy, 2, 23
Vinson, 17, 71

W

websites, 97
Western Canon University J.D. Salinger *Catcher in the Rye* Quad, 98

X

Xiong, C. V., 10

Z

"Zooey," 4

NOTES

NOTES

CliffsNotes

LITERATURE NOTES

Absalom, Absalom!
The Aeneid
Agamemnon
Alice in Wonderland
All the King's Men
All the Pretty Horses
All Quiet on the Western Front
All's Well & Merry Wives
American Poets of the 20th Century
American Tragedy
Animal Farm
Anna Karenina
Anthem
Antony and Cleopatra
Aristotle's Ethics
As I Lay Dying
The Assistant
As You Like It
Atlas Shrugged
Autobiography of Ben Franklin
Autobiography of Malcolm X
The Awakening
Babbit
Bartleby & Benito Cereno
The Bean Trees
The Bear
The Bell Jar
Beloved
Beowulf
The Bible
Billy Budd & Typee
Black Boy
Black Like Me
Bleak House
Bless Me, Ultima
The Bluest Eye & Sula
Brave New World
The Brothers Karamazov

The Call of the Wild & White Fang
Candide
The Canterbury Tales
Catch-22
Catcher in the Rye
The Chosen
The Color Purple
Comedy of Errors…
Connecticut Yankee
The Contender
The Count of Monte Cristo
Crime and Punishment
The Crucible
Cry, the Beloved Country
Cyrano de Bergerac
Daisy Miller & Turn…Screw
David Copperfield
Death of a Salesman
The Deerslayer
Diary of Anne Frank
Divine Comedy-I. Inferno
Divine Comedy-II. Purgatorio
Divine Comedy-III. Paradiso
Doctor Faustus
Dr. Jekyll and Mr. Hyde
Don Juan
Don Quixote
Dracula
Electra & Medea
Emerson's Essays
Emily Dickinson Poems
Emma
Ethan Frome
The Faerie Queene
Fahrenheit 451
Far from the Madding Crowd
A Farewell to Arms
Farewell to Manzanar
Fathers and Sons
Faulkner's Short Stories

Faust Pt. I & Pt. II
The Federalist
Flowers for Algernon
For Whom the Bell Tolls
The Fountainhead
Frankenstein
The French Lieutenant's Woman
The Giver
Glass Menagerie & Streetcar
Go Down, Moses
The Good Earth
The Grapes of Wrath
Great Expectations
The Great Gatsby
Greek Classics
Gulliver's Travels
Hamlet
The Handmaid's Tale
Hard Times
Heart of Darkness & Secret Sharer
Hemingway's Short Stories
Henry IV Part 1
Henry IV Part 2
Henry V
House Made of Dawn
The House of the Seven Gables
Huckleberry Finn
I Know Why the Caged Bird Sings
Ibsen's Plays I
Ibsen's Plays II
The Idiot
Idylls of the King
The Iliad
Incidents in the Life of a Slave Girl
Inherit the Wind
Invisible Man
Ivanhoe
Jane Eyre
Joseph Andrews
The Joy Luck Club
Jude the Obscure

Julius Caesar
The Jungle
Kafka's Short Stories
Keats & Shelley
The Killer Angels
King Lear
The Kitchen God's Wife
The Last of the Mohicans
Le Morte d'Arthur
Leaves of Grass
Les Miserables
A Lesson Before Dying
Light in August
The Light in the Forest
Lord Jim
Lord of the Flies
The Lord of the Rings
Lost Horizon
Lysistrata & Other Comedies
Macbeth
Madame Bovary
Main Street
The Mayor of Casterbridge
Measure for Measure
The Merchant of Venice
Middlemarch
A Midsummer Night's Dream
The Mill on the Floss
Moby-Dick
Moll Flanders
Mrs. Dalloway
Much Ado About Nothing
My Ántonia
Mythology
Narr. …Frederick Douglass
Native Son
New Testament
Night
1984
Notes from the Underground

The Odyssey
Oedipus Trilogy
Of Human Bondage
Of Mice and Men
The Old Man and
the Sea
Old Testament
Oliver Twist
The Once and
Future King
One Day in the Life of
Ivan Denisovich
One Flew Over the
Cuckoo's Nest
100 Years of Solitude
O'Neill's Plays
Othello
Our Town
The Outsiders
The Ox Bow Incident
Paradise Lost
A Passage to India
The Pearl
The Pickwick Papers
The Picture of
Dorian Gray
Pilgrim's Progress
The Plague
Plato's Euthyphro…
Plato's The Republic
Poe's Short Stories
A Portrait of the
Artist…
The Portrait of a Lady
The Power and
the Glory
Pride and Prejudice
The Prince
The Prince and
the Pauper
A Raisin in the Sun
The Red Badge of
Courage
The Red Pony
The Return of the
Native
Richard II
Richard III

The Rise of
Silas Lapham
Robinson Crusoe
Roman Classics
Romeo and Juliet
The Scarlet Letter
A Separate Peace
Shakespeare's
Comedies
Shakespeare's Histories
Shakespeare's
Minor Plays
Shakespeare's Sonnets
Shakespeare's Tragedies
Shaw's Pygmalion &
Arms…
Silas Marner
Sir Gawain…Green
Knight
Sister Carrie
Slaughterhouse-five
Snow Falling on Cedars
Song of Solomon
Sons and Lovers
The Sound and the Fury
Steppenwolf &
Siddhartha
The Stranger
The Sun Also Rises
T.S. Eliot's Poems &
Plays
A Tale of Two Cities
The Taming of the
Shrew
Tartuffe, Misanthrope…
The Tempest
Tender Is the Night
Tess of the D'Urbervilles
Their Eyes Were
Watching God
Things Fall Apart
The Three Musketeers
To Kill a Mockingbird
Tom Jones
Tom Sawyer
Treasure Island &
Kidnapped
The Trial

Tristram Shandy
Troilus and Cressida
Twelfth Night
Ulysses
Uncle Tom's Cabin
The Unvanquished
Utopia
Vanity Fair
Vonnegut's Works
Waiting for Godot
Walden
Walden Two
War and Peace
Who's Afraid of
Virginia…
Winesburg, Ohio
The Winter's Tale
The Woman Warrior
Worldly Philosophers
Wuthering Heights
A Yellow Raft in
Blue Water

Check Out the All-New CliffsNotes Guides

TECHNOLOGY TOPICS

Balancing Your Check-
book with Quicken
Buying and Selling
on eBay
Buying Your First PC
Creating a Winning
PowerPoint 2000
Presentation
Creating Web Pages
with HTML
Creating Your First
Web Page
Exploring the World
with Yahoo!
Getting on the Internet
Going Online with AOL
Making Windows 98
Work for You

Setting Up a
Windows 98
Home Network
Shopping Online Safely
Upgrading and
Repairing Your PC
Using Your First iMac
Using Your First PC
Writing Your First
Computer Program

PERSONAL FINANCE TOPICS

Budgeting & Saving
Your Money
Getting a Loan
Getting Out of Debt
Investing for the
First Time
Investing in
401(k) Plans
Investing in IRAs
Investing in
Mutual Funds
Investing in the
Stock Market
Managing Your Money
Planning Your
Retirement
Understanding
Health Insurance
Understanding
Life Insurance

CAREER TOPICS

Delivering a Winning
Job Interview
Finding a Job
on the Web
Getting a Job
Writing a Great Resume